SAFE PASSAGE INTO
THE TWENTY-FIRST CENTURY

SAFE PASSAGE INTO THE TWENTY-FIRST CENTURY

The United Nations' Quest for Peace, Equality, Justice, and Development

ROBERT MULLER
AND DOUGLAS ROCHE

A Global Education Associates Book

CONTINUUM • NEW YORK

1995

The Continuum Publishing Company
370 Lexington Avenue, New York, NY 10017

Printed in the United States of America

Library of Congress Cataloging-in-Publication Data

Muller, Robert, 1923-
    Safe passage into the twenty-first century ; the United
  Nations' quest for peace, equality, justice, and develop-
ment / Robert Muller and Douglas Roche
        p.   cm.
    "A Global Education Associates book."
    ISBN 0-8264-0866-4 (pbk. : alk. paper)
    1. United Nations. 2. United Nations—Anniversaries, etc.
  I. Roche, Douglas J.   II. Title.
  JX1977.M78   1995
  341.23—dc20   95-20380
                                                     CIP

Some day, when we have mastered
the winds, the tides, and gravity,
we will harness the energies of love.
Then, for the second time in the
history of the world, [the human
being] will have discovered fire.

— PIERRE TEILHARD DE CHARDIN

CONTENTS

INTRODUCTION

A Compass in Hand

A new phase of history has begun with the emergence of a global community.

Every day, newscasts bring further evidence of humankind's wrenching away from the bipolar world of the Cold War. The path forward is unclear, cluttered as it is with regional and ethnic conflict, poverty gaps, and huge migrations of peoples. Yet the advance toward globalization, led by the spectacular progress of technologies, is unmistakable.

It is now urgent to develop a vision of the world as a community. The old nationalisms are incapable of producing true human security in a world now interdependent in every major aspect of life. A new form of management of the planet, based first of all on cooperation, is essential. Such cooperation can open the way to the discovery of common values of East and West, North and South in the joint search for an enduring peace.

The expression of a new global ethic of sharing and stewardship might seem, to some, overly ambitious in a world still torn by the effects of long histories of greed and dominance. Yet agreement on common values for common survival is the most pressing challenge facing the international community.

This challenge comes into sharp focus at this moment, during the fiftieth anniversary of the United Nations, which itself occurs on the eve of the third millennium. The political and physical features of momentous change in the life of the planet coincide with the U.N. and millennium milestones.

Our objective in this book is to express our vision of the world community in terms related to the central political issues of our time. We want to meld our philosophy with the urgent political practicalities to offer a sort of blueprint on how to find safe passage into the twenty-first century.

For both of us, the United Nations has been our school and our place of work. For many years, we have dealt with ongoing U.N. issues—international development, disarmament, human rights, environmental protection, and, not least, administration. We have come to understand the vital importance of the U.N. as the centrepiece of the new world community. Thus, we have seized the opportunity offered by the fiftieth anniversary to assess the U.N.'s strengths and weaknesses in order to clarify its true role in the evolving human journey.

The U.N. has provided the framework for our discussion. In its deliberations aimed at producing a declaration for the fiftieth anniversary, the committee determined:

> The Charter needs to be applied to a new agenda. Such an agenda can be identified under the four main objectives the Charter lists as those which "we the peoples of the United Nations" are determined to achieve: peace, equality, justice and development.

We have taken these four elements—peace, equality, justice, and development—as the basis for our conversation. In this dialogue, we examined how each of the elements could be advanced in terms of common values. How can these goals be sought in cooperation rather than confrontation?

Political structures are slow to change and certainly sluggish in finding agreement on ways to move forward. The occasion of the fiftieth anniversary provides the impetus to advance reforms in world structures that will, in time, be deemed essential in the new millennium. Our vision of peace, equality, justice, and development is offered on the basis of political realities, but with a compass in hand for the way forward.

We had the inestimable benefit of serenity for our dialogue. It took place over several days at the University for Peace, a site in Costa Rica of pure enchantment. On a vast hill, it overlooks tropical-forested valleys in the central plains of Costa Rica. Flags of a number of nations fly at the entrance, near a monument erected to Mahatma Gandhi.

The University for Peace, established in 1980 by the United Nations, in addition to providing higher education for peace, promotes understanding, tolerance, and cooperation among peoples. The university projects the values of Costa Rica, the first demilitarized nation in the world. The university's motto is: "*Si vis pacem, para pacem.*" If you want peace, prepare for peace.

Enlightened realism is capable of producing a maturing process for all humanity. The U.N. expression of such an ethic, commonly held, can and must be helped to drive history forward. Time is of the essence.

CHAPTER I

Fifty Years of U.N. Experience

DOUGLAS ROCHE: Ten years ago, we held a dialogue on the eve of the fortieth anniversary of the United Nations, in which you said: "What we need in the United Nations is to look to the future, to focus on our beautiful planet and the very precious human species. We ought to put our hearts and minds into everything possible in order to enter the twenty-first century with more hope, security and development for all." Here we are ten years later on the occasion of the fiftieth anniversary and more particularly on the eve of the third millennium.

Instead of hope and security, we find the U.N. trying to pull itself together and facing a vote of confidence. I am looking at a headline in *The New York Times*: "U.N. Falters In Post-Cold War Peacekeeping But Sees Role As Essential." Because the U.N. could not bring peace to Bosnia, some people challenge its effectiveness, considering that the Cold War is over. The Security Council summit meeting that was to have kicked off the anniversary year was canceled because the permanent members didn't have anything to say that they could agree upon.

We also speak in the context of the growing amount of literature for the year 2000. For example, the distinguished statesman Conor Cruise O'Brien's book, *On the Eve of the Millennium*, takes a rather acerbic view of what he calls "the Guarded Palace"—that's the North cutting off the hands of those in the South.[1] Are we really as callous as that? On the other hand, we have the British Commission on the Millennium saying we should celebrate the year 2000 with "fizz, panache and excitement." The pope is planning a great eucharistic congress for the Holy land and Rome in the year 2000. We also have your own *Framework for Preparation for the Year 2000*, listing many ideas for action.[2] In this dialogue, I hope that we can project what is needed at this turning point in history to rekindle and rebuild the spirit of what Czech President Vaclav Havel referred to as "transcendence" in order to have the human being reach outward to connect in a manner of reconciliation with other humans and the earth itself. Either we take the transcendence route or we face extinction, given the massive powers of technology and the global problems running out of control. As we proceed into the year 2000, this is a good opportunity to look at human security issues so that we can determine whether there are reasons for hope.

ROBERT MULLER: First of all, the U.N. created such great expectations after World War II that people trumpeted it as a kind of a miracle organization. They wanted the U.N. to be able

---

1. Conor Cruise O'Brien, *On the Eve of the Millennium* (Concord, Ont.: Anansi, 1994).

2. Robert Muller, *Framework for Preparation for the Year 2000: The 21st Century and the Third Millennium* (Hamden, Conn.: Albert Einstein Institute/Quinnipac College Press, 1994).

to solve everything on Earth. This has not been possible because the Cold War intervened almost immediately after the creation of the U.N. The Cold War prevented the U.N. from having an effective military staff committee, composed of generals charged with building a world security system, after which they would have recommended disarmament. This idea died. The U.N.'s role was confined to peacekeeping and helping cope with the mounting refugees and other casualties of war. The U.N. was never allowed to prevent wars; moreover, it was excluded from some of the biggest conflicts of the past half century. For example, it was not allowed to intervene in Vietnam and Nicaragua for a long time.

Now that the Cold War is over, we look back to see whether there haven't been any achievements. Actually, when you look at the document, "The United Nations at 50: Recognizing the Achievements," the U.N. comes up with a lengthy list. I remember when I joined the U.N. in 1948, the number one problem was decolonization. I was told that it would take one hundred to one hundred and fifty years to solve, but it was done in forty years. One can close the Trusteeship Council today. Since we couldn't do much politically, we turned towards the economic field to address the problems of poor countries. We created, over the years, a total of thirty-two specialized agencies and world programs, such as the United Nations Development Program and the World Food Program which channels surpluses from the rich agricultural countries to the children and the poor in developing countries, and the like. We began to look at world trade. I spent several years trying to get a World Trade Organization established. Now a World Trade Organization has come into being. Similarly, we now have volumes of statistics on world population and on every global aspect of our planetary home and human family.

Also, we should not forget that, even on the political front, we have succeeded in not letting any of the local conflicts spill over into a world war: the Suez Canal, the Cuban Missile Crisis, hot spots which were very dangerous. We have done wonders. Even if we have not been able to solve all conflicts, we were able to put bandages on them.

DR: Perhaps "bandage" is a good word to use to express the dilemma that now comes sharply into focus. You speak of the Cold War that paralyzed the political relations between the East and West because of the arms race that the Cold War spawned. The Cold War also diverted from our consciousness the need to understand how we would all live in one world. When the Cold War suddenly ended, some anticipated an era of peace. Instead, we have seen one war after another as well as a widening gap between the North and the South. What has become clear is that there is a lack of a shared vision in the world between the East and West and the North and South.

So we have writers like Conor Cruise O'Brien saying that we are in this lifeboat, and the rich have filled the lifeboat and are chopping off the hands of the poor who are clamoring to get in. He uses as an example Haiti, saying that the operation to restore democracy in Haiti was a fraud, it was hypocrisy, that it was not designed primarily for democracy but to keep the flow of refugees from continuing into the United States. Other commentators are saying that the huge migrations of peoples spawned as a result of the increasing divisions between the North and the South are going to be met by resistance by the North because we do not care about them—and that this is perhaps the U.N.'s ultimate problem. Whatever bandages we are willing to put on to alleviate the worst forms of distress, we are not willing to make changes that will allow the weak and the vulnerable to achieve equitability with the rich and strong.

RM: There is already an incredible jump in human understanding when you speak about the East and West and the North and the South. There has never been talk about East and West and North and South in the entire human history. In my youth, the whole horizon was Germany and France. It was nations which were battling each other for little pieces of territory.

You speak about a global vision. Judging by my own experience in the U.N., I have seen movement towards a global vision, however awkward the movement. Until about 1968, the whole U.N. was concentrated on solving human problems. It was probably the most extraordinary humanistic period ever. Avoid wars, prolong life, save the children from early mortality, defend human rights, get the equality of the races, fight apartheid, obtain equality of the sexes, eradicate smallpox and other epidemics, increase longevity, feed the people, create a UNICEF for the children, think of the elderly. Someone should establish a list of everything that was thus tried for the first time at the global level in the whole human history.

And then around 1968 there was a change. It came from the government of Sweden, which was the first advanced industrial country to put before the U.N. the fact that acid rain was destroying forests and that their lakes were becoming polluted. The scientists then responded and UNESCO held the first World Biosphere Conference. It turned out to be a flop. Why? Because there was not a head of State on the planet who knew what the biosphere was. So the Swedes came to the United Nations Economic and Social Council and said, look, we have to warn the world that something is going wrong. The result was the first world conference on this issue in Stockholm in 1972. We had to find a word to characterize it. I remember I was for pollution, the scientists were for biosphere, and someone came up with the word "environment."

The Environment Conference in 1972 in Stockholm was a historic turning point because, since then, U.N. efforts have been expanded to humanity's connection with the planet, without having solved all the earlier problems. There is still poverty, still sexual discrimination, still racial discrimination, although apartheid now has been solved.

DR: Still violence.

RM: Yes, violence and other accumulated problems. But we came up with something new, namely, the recognition that we have to take care of what is around us, namely nature, the elements of the Earth. The Stockholm conference in 1972 was attended by only two heads of state, Olof Palme, the head of Sweden, and Mrs. Indira Gandhi of India. When the Earth Summit met again 20 years later in Rio de Janeiro, it had 103 heads of state and thousands of representatives of non-governmental organizations. When the Stockholm meeting was held, there was not a single environment ministry on the planet. Today, there is not a single country without a minister of the environment.

Around 1980, we received a warning from climatologists who told us the climate of the planet will deteriorate if we continue along the present path. If we continue to emit carbon dioxide into the air, by about the year 2025 the currents of the oceans will change direction and will become irreversible for thousands of years. That led to the U.N. World Climate Conference. Since 1980, we have entered a new period where the earth is number one and humans are number two, to the point that people want world population and overconsumption to diminish. This is where we are today. In the short period of fifty years, there have been quantum changes in emphasis in trying to find our way on the planet. As a matter of fact, I have recommended that in 1998, thirty years after the 1968 Biosphere Conference, there should be another world conference on the biosphere because I think the concept of the sphere of life—where we are part of nature and not different from nature—is the correct attitude and should be emphasized.

DR: I feel about the United Nations at fifty the way that I did at the fortieth anniversary when people said, well, it's forty years old, it's having a mid-life crisis. And I said, what do you mean, "a mid-life crisis"? The U.N. is still in its infancy! The reason that I took on the role of chairman of the Canadian committee for the fiftieth anniversary was because I am trying to prepare the way for the seventy-fifth anniversary. That is why I consider the activities of our youth committee among the most important things that we are doing. We are holding conferences with youth at the university level along with special leadership training institutes for senior high school students, the cream of the crop across the country. Every elementary and high school in Canada will observe United Nations Day on October 24, 1995 with a great run-up of material, teaching guides, and materials that we are producing for teachers.

We must expand the intellectual basis of understanding and support for the United Nations. When I tell my students about the United Nations, it takes a long time just to give the basic facts of what the thirty-two specialized agencies and world programs are doing. People don't know about this wide range of activity. What the Canadian Committee wants to do is to increase the understanding as a means of raising the global consciousness so that there will be a better appreciation of the full potential of the U.N. The Secretary-General is promoting the wide range of activities around the world in educational activities, publications, film and television programming, radio media campaigns, conferences and seminars, along with exhibits, concerts, and other public events. I would say this enormous range of activity about the United Nations is one of the reasons why we should increase our hope that the U.N. can continue to be developed.

RM: As an old United Nations official, I would like to reminisce about this. I remember the tenth anniversary of the United Nations, which was an event practically limited to the United States. It was a meeting in San Francisco. President Eisenhower came. It was a good celebration, but beyond that there was very little. It was not celebrated around the world at all. Then we had the twenty-fifth anniversary, in which I was involved because I was the executive director for U Thant, the secretary-general. With colleagues like Ralph Bunche, we took the occasion of the twenty-fifth anniversary to have the secretary-general make a number of stock-taking speeches on all the great aspects of the world's problems and the role of the United Nations. We also had a news conference, which involved young people. We asked them: "What do you see for the future of the world?" Governments were a little scared of this conference because youth has always advanced new ideas. So the twenty-fifth was much more important than the tenth.

The fortieth was a big jump ahead because, for the first time, national committees were formed. Secretary-General Perez de Cuellar sent a note to all heads of government, asking them to assess what the past forty years had meant to their country, and to look into the future. This fiftieth is the biggest of all. Major speeches have been given by Boutros-Ghali. We have a General Assembly committee and national committees in practically every nation. The specialized agencies are involved. Young people are involved. Children are involved. All the Nobel Peace Prize winners will meet in San Francisco to commemorate the signing of the Charter and give their views of how to develop a peaceful future. On October 24 in New York, many heads of state will gather.

We have progressed from a small tenth anniversary to a significant milestone. This can become bigger still because of the arrival of the third millennium in five years. The United Nations should adopt a resolution to celebrate the year 2000 world-wide and the General Assembly establish a committee to prepare this celebration. Also, each country should create a national committee to prepare for the year 2000.

Celebrations are a fundamental human means to feel together, to think together, to assess together, to dream together. You have family birthdays, marriages, religious ceremonies, saints' days, Christmas. Then when the nation state came into existence, we began to have the national holidays. And we have now a new phenomenon, namely, in the last few years, the birth of world celebrations. We have now a total of thirty-four days in the year when there are world celebrations—a world population day, a world no-tobacco day, an international day of the family, a world health day, a world day for water, a world day of the elderly, an international women's day, an international day of peace, etc. These days make people begin to feel together.

DR: Celebration is an important aspect of human life. It is not inappropriate to celebrate the fiftieth anniversary. That being said, it isn't exactly a celebratory motivation that the secretary-general has in mind nor, indeed, do I. I think that it is important to look ahead to what the United Nations can and must become. And that gets into the reform of the United Nations, which the secretary-general has also asked for. When one considers reform, there are two or three areas that immediately come to mind. The first is the expansion of the Security Council beyond its present permanent five membership, the United States, Russia, United

Kingdom, France, and China to a more representative body that would include at least a state from Africa, a state from South America, and more states from Asia. This is now a subject of great controversy at the United Nations.

So, too, is the subject of expanding peacekeeping into a permanent peacekeeping force. I am pleased that Canada has launched a formal study of what is involved in having a permanent U.N. peacekeeping force, especially as you look at the four dimensions as outlined in Boutros-Ghali's *An Agenda for Peace*, which are preventive diplomacy, peacemaking, peacekeeping, and peacebuilding.[3] It is the peacemaking aspect that now needs to be studied out of the experiences in Somalia and Bosnia, which have soured many people on the U.N.'s ability to bring peace. A stronger U.N. of the future requires the expansion of the Security Council permanent membership, a permanent peacekeeping force, and a higher-level body promoting international development. These areas of reform of the U. N. that are now opened up are very important and call for a deeper educational base of those who are making policies as well as publics to support these policies.

RM: Canada provides a good example. So does Costa Rica, where the National Committee for the Fiftieth Anniversary is headed by former President Rodrigo Carazo, who founded the University for Peace. Costa Rica shows other countries that they, too, can demilitarize. Panama has now followed its example. President Carazo has proposed that the whole month of October 1995 should be a world armistice all around the world as a gift to the United Nations for its anniversary.

---

3. Boutros Boutros-Ghali, *An Agenda for Peace* (New York: United Nations Department of Public Information, 1995).

DR: There is no doubt that the accumulation of information about the planet fostered by the U.N. conferences over the past twenty or so years has been enormous. We now see ourselves. We are like the astronauts in outer space sending back the photograph of the beautiful, blue, shimmering globe in which we see ourselves for the first time. My great-grandfather came on a boat from Ireland to a strange place called Canada. What did he know about Latin America or Africa? Here we are, three generations later, with this comprehensive understanding of the world.

That highlights my point that we can certainly credit the United Nations with having fostered our knowledge of ourselves as world citizens. But it hasn't been able to reconcile the greed factor that is at the basis of domination and violence and wars and aggression. The dilemma of the end of the Cold War is that these are now pointed up: the pulling back into ethnic and tribal hatreds unleashing atrocities that defy description. This has been a very demoralizing aspect for much of humanity, seeing that we can't really "make it" after all as a human race. This has contributed to the demoralizing of the United Nations.

I have read all the documentation concerning what the United Nations has done in the past fifty years. And I second you completely in affirming that there is not a human being on the planet who has not been affected in some manner by the United Nations. That isn't the point here. The point is whether or not the reasons we adduce for hope of continued elevation of the human family on its journey through time are sound. Is the greed factor that has dominated human history going to prove too much, in the end, to allow the uninterrupted development of humanity?

RM: My family history was deeply affected by the wars between France and Germany. My grandfather changed nationality five times between these two countries. All the horrors I saw in the World War II! I just cannot believe what I see today. I cannot believe that I can go back to Europe and freely cross the border between Belgium, Germany, France, Holland, Luxembourg as I did last year. No border controls any more. The border which I saw and which created so many wars has disappeared. We are a united Europe somewhat like the United States. There has been an incredible change of attitude in the world towards war. You don't have any war ministries anymore. They now call themselves ministries of defense.

I worked with three U.N. secretaries-general and whenever we were invited to a dinner or a luncheon with a head of state, I always managed to put a little question: "Do you think that you could become famous by waging and winning a war?" They all looked at me as if I were crazy. Then I had another question: "Do you think you could become famous by being a peacemaker and getting the Nobel Peace Prize?" This brought smiles. If you bring together today all the heads of states, you won't find an Alexander the Great, a Caesar, or Napoleon any more. Modern leaders seldom think of aggressing other countries anymore.

DR: What about Saddam Hussein?

RM: So what? That is one case out of 185 nations. You cannot take only one example. You cannot point to only one wound. If I break a toe, it doesn't mean that my entire being is affected.

DR: Defense departments all over the world, particularly the major powers, express fears there will be more Saddam Husseins. That apparently justifies their continuation of high spending for defense in the post–Cold War era.

RM: So we have to deal with this problem. But we do not have to deal with any more Hitlers, Mussolinis, war lords, Napoleons, Alexanders the Great, Caesars, and other conquerors. This period is over. Now they call themselves "defense." All right. They speak about "security." Let us come up with a new system of security. If you look at the conflicts today, out of seventy-two conflicts, you have only three international ones, and they are on the way to being solved. Even the Middle East is making progress. What do we have now? Internal conflicts. The United Nations has never previously been asked to intervene in an internal conflict.

DR: It's in the charter not to intervene.

RM: Suddenly, the United Nations is asked to get into Bosnia, into Rwanda. And we have no experience. But I will make a prediction. In a number of years, the U. N. will have the same experience and the same success with internal conflicts as it had with international conflicts. If I were the secretary-general, one of the first things I would do is create a department dealing with ethnic and religious conflicts. No one has much expertise in the United Nations with internal, ethnic, and religious conflicts. We have a lot of experience in international conflicts but not with these new types of conflicts. Let us not forget that countries like Yugoslavia (the Slavs of the south) and many African countries, due to colonialism, are pretty incoherent countries without an ethnic, national unity.

DR: Let me come to my central problem from the avenue that you opened up a moment ago by talking about security. Indeed, that's one more thing we have the United Nations to thank for: the wide definition of security given by the Security Council summit of

January 1992, that security today can no longer be measured in military terms, but must also be measured in economic and social development, environmental protection, and advancement of human rights and humanitarian considerations. All those things make a wide, integrated agenda for security.

As we try to apply this now, we come to grips with the fundamental problem we have faced since coming out of the cave—the domination by the strong over the weak. And the reluctance of nations to put resources into the development of children, women, to advance the whole economic and social agenda. There is still resistance to the fundamental concept that people have a right to essential life-sustaining goods. The integrity of the human being, which everyone has by virtue of being human, is not respected by the strong. As I said, we had this problem coming out of the cave, but now in this postmodern age it seems to me that in the problems of common survival, as severe as they are, the rich will continue to dominate the poor. We've seen it in the statistics of the last thirty years. The richest fifth of humanity has an income now sixty times greater than the poorest fifth of humanity. Migrations are increasing. The populations of refugees, what's been called the poor nomads, are adversely affected by the results of aggression. The United Nations cannot solve this problem by itself because the major powers are driven by economic considerations in which the poor continue to be dominated by the interests of the rich.

RM: I am going to make another prediction: all the big powers are going to die. The first one that has ended is the Soviet Union. In the whole history of humankind, no empire has survived that did not adapt to the fundamental currents of evolution. This is why the Soviets collapsed. On the fortiethth anniversary of the U.N., the Soviets established a committee to review the entire postwar policy of the Soviet Union. I remember getting the first notices that they had come to the conclusion that all their post-war foreign policy was wrong.

Now the United States and the Europeans still believe that they are right. Look what's happening in a country like France. There are 12 million Arabs in France. Immigration is taking place. The Mexicans are in California. The Nicaraguan migrants come here to Costa Rica. This is the new migration. The big powers cannot stop these migrations because they need cheap labor.

Practically every population in the western world is declining. This is the beginning of their end because the overconsumption and materialistic life which we promote as being the best thing on earth is going to collapse. I don't see many people laugh in the Western countries any more. Young people go to universities to study and then find no jobs. So the major powers shouldn't think that they are so great and so rich and so advanced. They must adapt to evolution and this is why it would be in their interest to take the United Nations utmost seriously as the point of convergence of all these world trends, as the transcending, metabiological organ of human evolution, and bring forth a philosophy and vision of what the world should be tomorrow. This is the issue which is now apparent at the end of the second millennium.

DR: My vision of this new world starts from a recognition that a new global ethic is required precisely because all the political and economic and social policymakers and physical scientists have had their day and have not been able to solve these essential problems that persist even into the new age. For me, it is not a technological crisis that we face but a spiritual crisis. All my experience as a parliamentarian, as a diplomat, as a journalist traveling widely through all areas of the developing world as well as the developed over four decades has convinced me that the problems we are talking about are most of all ethical problems.

They have to do with how we are going to treat one another on this shrinking planet. I return to my thesis that we haven't done a very good job of this all through the ages and through the two millennia that are part of our legacy. What is it that can produce some hope in people that we can overcome the fundamental factors of greed that have divided humanity on our journey through time and are exacerbated in this new era, which is fraught with danger with the breakup of societies over resource allocations and the continuation of aggression? The unwillingness of the major powers to fund the United Nations to empower it to take those steps toward a more equitable kind of world adds to the danger. When it comes down to the fundamental spiritual value of our humanity, whether we are Muslim, Hindu, Christian, or Jew, there are still deep animosities continuing to divide us.

RM: In my writings on the United Nations and spirituality I deal with this and all the voices that came from Hammarskjold, U Thant, Perez de Cuellar and many others who stressed the need for a spiritual renaissance on this planet. And it is coming. Look at all the religious wars we had during the Middle Ages. Killing in the name of God was the rule. Religion was discredited to the point that the French Revolution abolished religions as the biggest troublemakers. Even today, many regard religions as troublemakers. That is why the common values between all religions should be expressed. They should cooperate in order to work on common values such as faith, prayer, compassion, charity, forgiveness, etc. With the Cold War over and the opposition to religion and spirituality ended in the former communist countries of Eastern Europe, we can move, we must move, to a spiritual renaissance, to a global spirituality.

DR: What makes you confident that there will be a spiritual renaissance? What do you see in the human character that is suddenly changed just because we are in a postmodern era?

RM: Because people are tired of the materialistic, noisy life of today. They are not satisfied. They are not really happy. They are not given a view of the universe in which they live and a true meaning of life. And this is why more people become monks or solitary people, or go into meditation. I don't know if anyone has evaluated the number of Yoga courses, the impact of Buddhism and of holistic health around the world. It is substantial. People are finding answers in Oriental mystics that they don't find in going to the supermarket, to the movies or watching television. Many people are returning to religions and spirituality, the same way as they are returning to nature. Look at how many people are again planting trees, are taking care of the environment. It is incredible.

Looking at the next century and what can be done, I would like to see a U.N. commission created to deal only with the future. Like the American Iroquois, we would ask the question: what will be the effect of such and such action on the seventh generation? We do not even think of the next generation. True, we have a Commission on Education in the Twenty-First century, a World Commission on Global Governance. We had a World Conference on Human Rights to tell us what human rights in the twenty-first century should be. We have *An Agenda for Peace* by the secretary-general. We have *Agenda 21* from the Earth Summit.[4] Never has humanity prepared itself for a new century and millennium as we are doing now. This is why I'm very optimistic. We must

---

4. *Agenda Twenty-One* (New York: United Nations Department of Public Information, 1992).

put all this together and show the promises of a positive future. This will give an uplift to humanity. At the U.N. we must be global doctors and not consider the case of humanity as hopeless. We must do our very best and at least learn together how to do better next time. We are still in a global kindergarten. That has always been my attitude at the United Nations. Unfortunately, the media focus on the negative.

DR: People are subjected to the world as it is presented by the media, which has its own standards for the depiction of what is going on. I have often told my students, you cannot judge the tremendous amount of creativity in the world by looking at the news because by definition they are dwelling on the confrontational, which is usually highly negative.

I come out of a parliamentary environment where politicians are dealing with what they claim are the crises of the day and the fact that most people are interested in what is affecting their business or their family today or this week. The fewest number of people are interested in global issues twenty-five years from now. If we had put into political practice, through public policy formation, policies to deal with the environment, to deal with disarmament, to deal with development twenty-five years ago, all those agendas that are at the heart of the global security agenda today would be greatly advanced. Similarly, it is our inability politically to look forward in public policy formation twenty-five years from now that will make the problems we are talking about even worse in the next twenty-five year period. Politicians are driven by the moment and the media manipulates the moment. We have not yet overcome the narrowness of the political systems that are holding back the development of the United Nations as you would have it.

RM: Again, I have to put an optimistic note into this. It is not because the majority of politicians are narrow-minded that a person must also be narrow-minded. I will not accept this. It is not because others are hopeless that I will be hopeless, too. If I'm only one voice in the desert, I will be that voice. I'll give you a good example of a friend of mine who had the courage to be a voice in an impossible situation. It was Robert Schuman from Alsace Lorraine who decided to reconcile France and Germany. When he became minister for foreign affairs, what did he do? He created a Coal and Steel Community to show that you could use the coal of the Ruhr and the iron ore of Lorraine to make the two countries work together. This was followed by a European Economic Community and culminated in a Political Community. It took almost forty years, but today we have a united Europe. It was due to his persistence and against all odds of an incipient opposition and hatred. He created European institutions as Benjamin Franklin created American institutions. Borders have disappeared, and other countries are ready to join the united Europe. I'm very glad to be a member of the canonization committee of Robert Schuman, because the man was a saint. After Coal and Steel, after the Economic Community, after the Political Community, he wanted to create a European spiritual community. I want to help this to be achieved. We must embark upon the same "Mission Impossible" for the world. We are in need of political saints.

DR: I have to make a small correction in something you said in your last comment. I do not consider you one voice in the desert or in the wilderness—not at all. I consider you a leader of those who are thinking their way into the future. While we are enjoying the solitude that this moment gives us, we are by no means alone. There are thousands, one could say millions, of people in the world who are as oriented and as concerned as we are about this idea of the sharing values of humanity going forward. Ten years ago, there were about 100 million people who were affected by the non-governmental organization movement. Today there are 250 million people. The synergy of energy that brought down the Berlin Wall was the synergy of energy that we saw in Rio with the Earth Summit. It is reflected by the women at the Beijing Ccnference. This is a manifestation of the growth in the horizontalization of leadership that is taking place in the world today. It may be God's way of giving us a new kind of leadership, since we haven't had sufficient vertical leadership. Of course, there are people like us. What we want to do is to give them reasons for hope so that they will continue to use their energy flowing out into multiple avenues. My point here is that this public is held back by a political process that is focused too inwardly. You speak of Schuman and the spiritual community that he foresaw. Of course, this is what we want to aim for. But when you talk to the average politician, not the people we have been talking about here in the horizontalization of leadership, about a spiritual community they say, "Oh, that's wonderful, but meanwhile I have to deal with this problem of today, and I haven't got time to talk about spirituality."

RM: I sometimes receive letters from people who tell me, Mr. Muller, you spoke in such and such a place, you had a few words with me after your speech and since then, my life has changed. I am very happy because now I do positive things. And this helps. If one could convince the leaders of nations, it would be even better. One has to try. Some of them are listening. Others don't as yet. You're quite right: the leaders of nations may come together, but when they go home they have a strike, an election, inflation, or other immediate problems and they forget about the world and the United Nations. At least they have representatives sitting in the U.N. and the secretary-general who can tell them what is truly needed in the world. Someday, with the progress of global education, we will have different leaders, politicians, and media. I sometimes dream of seeing this University for Peace become the first school for heads of states of this planet.

DR: Once again, the fundamental divisions of humanity that prevent the U.N. from solving the major problems are constraints in preparing a declaration to mark the U.N.'s fiftieth anniversary. It was very difficult even to get an acceptable theme for the United Nations. Some wanted to have "The United Nations for Peace and Justice and Development" but because of the reluctance of some states in the North to expose themselves to precise questions on what they mean by justice and development, the preparatory committee agreed to the theme "The United Nations for a Better World." We all want a better world, but it is *how* that world will become better that the U. N. must address. The committee did agree on four "elements," "peace," "equality," "justice," and "development." I propose that we look at these four elements in the context of what we have been saying about the holistic nature of education and the integrated agenda for global security. What common values underlie the search for peace, equality, justice, and development today? How can these goals be sought in cooperation rather than confrontation?

RM: One of the reasons the U.N. agreed to the four concepts of peace, equality, justice, and development is because those words are in the U.N. charter. It is always easier to refer to something which has been agreed upon in the past. You don't have to redebate it. I would not have objections to the general theme, "The United Nations for a Better World," because I think we can show that the proper development of peace, equality, justice, and development can lead to a vision of the correct relationship between humans and the planet. We can transcend today's problems into a more elevated common denominator for humanity. In the complexity of the present world, from the sea of information and activities, the U.N., like Plato in Athens, is trying to extract the "essence." The fundamental values, the ethics of our mysterious journey in the universe.

CHAPTER 2

Peace: Curing the Sickness of Violence

DR: The U.N. committee planning a declaration for the fiftieth anniversary began with these words: "Peace and security over-arch all other activities and goals, but peace is shaped by a complex of factors: economic and social deprivation; ethnic/historic/nationalist/territorial factors; social injustice; weapon balances; and involuntary movements of peoples." I want to concentrate on the words "weapon balances."

The end of the section on peace says the role of the U.N. in developing, safeguarding, and monitoring treaties relating to disarmament, arms reduction, and non-proliferation of weapons must be further developed. Actually, it is the by-passing of the U.N. that has caused the major problem in finding the surest route to peace, which is the elimination of nuclear weapons. The two superpowers did the negotiating themselves on reductions of nuclear weapons and have resisted and continue to resist the United Nations playing a vigorous role in fulfilling the conditions set out in the Final Document of the First Special Session of Disarmament in 1978, which called for "general and complete disarmament under effective international control."

The outrageous conduct of the two superpowers, the U.S. and the former Soviet Union, abetted by the three other nuclear powers, the U.K., France, and China, in building up stocks of strategic nuclear weapons during the Cold War, flouted the U.N. There were some 56,400 strategic weapons in 1988 at the height of the Cold War. I have been to Hiroshima. I have seen the destruction caused by one weapon. I have interviewed the survivors. I have seen the artifacts in the museums, and I am so conscious of the result of one nuclear weapon, not to mention Nagasaki, that I am filled with rage at the idea that the rest of the world has been held hostage by the nuclear weapons powers. When one considers that the nuclear powers are, at one and the same time, the five permanent members of the Security Council, there is a great deal for those nations to account for.

Having expressed this very large negative, I want to turn my vision to a future in which it is not only desirable but feasible to obtain a world free of nuclear weapons. The end of the Cold War has presented us with a new opportunity to achieve the goal that the U.N. set out in the Final Document. It's an irony that the charter of the United Nations is silent on the question of nuclear weapons. We know the reason is that the charter was signed before the first nuclear explosion. It is in consequence of the silence of the charter on nuclear weapons that the Non-Proliferation Treaty achieves all the more importance because the NPT promised a nuclear-weapons-free world. A great struggle preceded the indefinite extension of the NPT, revolving around the refusal of the nuclear powers to consider elimination of nuclear weapons in specific time frames. They continue to be charged by a number of important states with fomenting a two-class world for the twenty-first century: those who have nuclear weapons, maintaining them as the currency of power, while proscribing nuclear weapons for the rest of the world. This is not acceptable to many states.

The search for global security, the struggle over an integrated agenda, is impeded by the maintenance of nuclear weapons. We must find a way to make it possible for the nuclear weapons powers to proceed to the fulfillment of that which they have committed themselves to by their signatures on the Non-Proliferation Treaty. That is why the role of the United Nations is so important. It's not yet generally appreciated that a fourth special session on disarmament has been scheduled for 1997. Thus we have a route to pursuance of the Final Document, a route to accomplishing, through specific time frames, the elimination of nuclear weapons. The agenda for common security, the wide agenda for peace, the quest for a new world order, is incompatible with the maintenance of nuclear weapons. Nuclear weapons are the central obstacle to the world of peace that we seek.

RM: There is yet another development which must be watched very carefully. I received from scientists indications that the scientific world continues to develop all kinds of strange new weapons. In particular, new kinds of rays are being tested in the Arctic, which could have the effect of changing the climate of the earth. So, we might have another type of arms as damaging to the total planetary environment as the nuclear ones. Also with the end of the Cold War, the United States and Russia could have gone back to the situation in 1944 with a renewed plan to organize the world rationally and in peace under the United Nations. I was always impressed with the original plan to entrust the military staff committee of the Security Council with the task of creating a world security system, and then to take up disarmament. That was the way of proceeding correctly. We cannot have disarmament if we don't have a world security system. But as soon as the Cold War broke out, the efforts were abandoned. I wish that on the occasion of the fiftieth anniversary the military staff will be reactivated at the chiefs of staff level. This way exists in the charter and should be revived.

But what is happening in the U.S., the biggest power on earth with the most sophisticated weapons? Their view is now: "We're in charge of the world to make it a better place. We will make sure there will be no dictators anywhere, that there will be parliaments everywhere, that there will be democracy and the type of governmental system of freedom which we have in the United States. We cannot rely on the United Nations because you never know what will happen. It is too big a risk. We are in charge."

I think this is the mentality in Washington. It is not illogical. It is pretty logical.

DR: It's logical from their point of view.

RM: From their point of view, yes.

DR: It's not logical from my point of view.

RM: Exactly, but I'm just saying that this is the first obstacle before we can even discuss nuclear weapons. As far as Russia is concerned, if the United States had said, we have a completely new vision of the world, we are proud to have the United Nations on our soil, we created the United Nations and will use it to build a new world order as was planned in 1944—the Russians probably would have gone along. Now they have strong hesitations and they are beginning to behave again as another big power.

DR: You have mentioned the effect of the continued moderniza-
tion leading into the third age of nuclear weapons as a threat to
the environment. We're quite familiar with the previous nuclear
winter projections. I think that the major powers want nuclear
weapons and want to maintain them because that is the way they
effect their power, their control over the international agenda.
The United Kingdom and France would certainly be greatly
reduced in their status today without nuclear weapons. In the
case of the United States, I think what you said about their desire
to effect good through their control, from their point of view,
may be logical, but what it is doing is causing other nations to
resent this control and to try to catch up. The consequence of that
will be that the Non-Proliferation Treaty, even though it has been
extended indefinitely, will not be able to stop the horizontal proliferation of nuclear weapons in the twenty-first century.

What amazes me is that the public is asleep on this issue. The
public thinks that, because there has been nuclear disarmament
between the Soviet Union and now Russia and the United States
in bringing down numbers within the strategic categories, the
problem has gone away. They don't seem to realize that given a
perfect fulfillment of the existing treaties—START I and START
II, the latter not yet even ratified—we would have in the year
2003 still nearly twelve thousand nuclear weapons retained by
those two countries. Not to mention the stocks of the other three.
This is not an incentive to the other nations that are the near-
nuclears to stop their quest for nuclear weapons.

I agree with the Foreign Minister of India, who, at the First
Committee in the 1994 session of the U.N. General Assembly, said
that even with the deceleration by the two major countries, all
this will still lead to the two countries holding weapons by the
thousands, each ten to fifty times the size of the bomb dropped
on Hiroshima. The Rajiv Gandhi Foundation and the Gorbachev

Foundation, to name just two of the important intellectual centres for peace, are saying very clearly that nuclear weapons remain the greatest threat to the security of nations and to the survival of human civilization. They say that failure to control and eliminate them could result in the emergence of a dangerous international environment composed both of nuclear-armed criminal and terrorist groups and a score or more of nuclear-weapon states ceaselessly competing with one another in futile efforts to maximize their own security. The public is asleep on this issue. There are no more demonstrations. People think the problem has gone away.

We are now on the eve of the millennium. The 1995 extension of the Non-Proliferation Treaty certainly did not resolve this issue satisfactorily. We have the U.N. General Assembly's Fourth Special Session on Disarmament coming up in 1997. I want to know how we can increase the United Nations' role in pursuing nuclear disarmament to abolition.

RM: Well, why not create an Independent World Commission of Eminent Persons for the Abolition of all Nuclear Weapons, headed by a prominent head of state. It would declare the destruction of all nuclear weapons as the top item on the agenda of world affairs. It would devise a bold, vast, water-tight strategy dealing with all regions and elements of the planet. The Antarctic is already denuclearized. So are the moon and outer space. So is all Latin America by the Treaty of Tlatelolco, thanks to our U.N. colleague and Nobel Peace Prize Winner Alfonso Garcia Roblas, from Mexico. The just created Independent World Commission for the Seas and Oceans under the chairmanship of the president of Portugal, Mario Soares, could take up the denuclearization of all seas and oceans as the priority item on their agenda. Public opinion could be strongly reactivated on the issue. British and French citizens could introduce recourses against their governments in the European Court of Justice, claiming that they have the fundamental human right to live in countries without nuclear arms. This new human right should be taken up in the U.N. Human Rights Commission. There are hosts of things such a world commission could do during these crucial years on the eve of a new century and millennium.

U.S. General Charles A. Horner, former Commander U.S. Space Command, retired, should be invited to be a member of this world commission. His statement that "the nuclear weapon is obsolete. I want to get rid of them all" would highly qualify him for membership.

DR: You recognize the problem that the United Nations faces in trying to effect disarmament in the face of the major powers. But nuclear weapons cannot be abolished until we cure the reason for nuclear weapons. Nuclear weapons are not about an enmity of one people against another. Nuclear weapons are not just instruments of death. What nuclear weapons are about is the sickness within humanity that produces violence. Until we get the sickness cured, we will not be able to get sufficient confidence in the political machinery to effect nuclear disarmament.

Before we leave this subject, I want to note in passing that the non-aligned states did produce a draft text for the fiftieth anniversary declaration. Their document was summarily cast aside because it was specific in several areas, of which nuclear weapons is one. The non-aligned document said: "We consider unacceptable the developing, producing and stockpiling of nuclear weapons and other weapons of mass destruction as well as strategic doctrines based on the use or threat of use of such weapons." That idea didn't go very far in the committee because the only way they can get consensus in a declaration is to keep it on the general or, some would even say, vague side.

The minute you go into the specifics of a time line for nuclear weapons reduction, the resistance of the powerful is uppermost. At the First Committee in 1994, a new resolution was introduced by Mexico and supported by ten other leading non-aligned states which called for a step-by-step reduction of nuclear weapons to zero within a time period of about ten years. The very idea of a step-by-step phased elimination of nuclear weapons to zero was resisted by the nuclear powers. The United States attacked the resolution for its "academic design." France said it "only serves the objectives of countries that cannot accept the new realities and seeks to place all the burden on nuclear weapon states." The vote on this was ninety-one in favor, twenty-four opposed and thirty abstaining. This reinforces the reasons why education and the development of global consciousness to raise a new global ethic must eventually make itself heard and felt in the corridors of power.

RM: Another way to foster change in the world leading realistically to a reduction of nuclear weapons, would be for a country like the United States to have the vision of a Franklin D. Roosevelt and to do exactly what Roosevelt did at the time when we were in the worst period of history, when everybody was fed up with the war, and when he came up with a new vision. The new vision would be: "We are proud, as the United States, to have contributed to the birth of a new world order by creating the United Nations. We were to a certain extent responsible for World War II because we did not ratify the League of Nations. We didn't want to make this mistake again. We created the United Nations and are proud that it represents a new opportunity for the world. Now that the Cold War is over, we are going to strengthen the United Nations as the principal way to a peaceful and disarmed world order. And we will take the first step with the destruction of all nuclear weapons." The whole world would applaud such a speech by the U.S. President at the fiftieth anniversary. Unfortunately, the U.S. has not taken such a decision. They have, in fact, excluded it. As long as one of the biggest countries on earth doesn't even think of a world order that could be different from their own domination of the world, a fundamental impediment to peace, security, and disarmament remains.

Perhaps the new world order of tomorrow will not come from the U.S. and the United Nations. It might come from Europe, which had the courage to define a new system where national sovereignties have at least been reduced to a certain extent. You now have a European parliament to which parliamentarians are directly elected by the people. The European Commission has $70 billion of common resources. There is a European Court in which a state can be condemned for its behavior towards another member or citizens. What Jean Monnet and Robert Schuman have achieved in Europe is incredible. It took them forty years, but it is now there. With other nations joining, the union might reach from Great Britain to Russia and the north of China. The temptation of an alliance between Asia and Europe (Eurasia), would isolate the United States. I warned President Bush about this, when he was a delegate to the U.N. Why don't you organize the Americas? I hear Latin American countries dreaming of joining the European community via Spain and Portugal. Why is your mind always in the Soviet Union, in China, and in Japan, when you have the richest hemisphere of North and South America?" At least NAFTA was born as a beginning, and the heads of states of the American countries are meeting every year. The European example will be followed by others. It is irreversible. There are twelve regional communities in the works around the world.

If the United Nations is kept hanging in the air, criticized systematically by the extreme right of the United States; if the

United States withholds its contributions to the U.N; if the United States does not return to UNESCO—I would put my entire weight behind the European Union as the cradle of the world community of tomorrow, the United States being hopeless as it was after World War I.

Jean Monnet was very clear in his prophecy: "Have I said clearly enough that the community we created is not an end in itself? It is a process of change, continuing in that same process which in an earlier period produced our national form of life. The sovereign nations of the past can no longer solve the problems of the present: they cannot ensure their own progress or control their own future. And the community itself is only a stage on the way of the organized world of tomorrow."

There must be a new world political organization. I recommend for the fiftieth anniversary that we should create at least a consultative parliamentary assembly for the United Nations, so that parliamentarians would be able to know what is going on in the United Nations and have a voice of the people in it.

DR: There is a role for the United Nations in disarmament, and that is to increase its efforts at promoting verification mechanisms, and in expanding its peacekeeping operations in the light of *An Agenda for Peace*. Before we get to that, I want to conclude this section of our conversation on this note. If the United Nations cannot be effective in nuclear disarmament at this stage, surely the U. N. can increase its efforts via the U.N. Register on Arms to stop the arms trade. Here we are still in the beginning stages of identifying, through methods of transparency, conventional armaments in some categories. But the Arms Register still does not deal with weapons of mass destruction, and it does not make mandatory the reporting. It does not control the arms trade which, sad to say, is expanding into the South because the northern markets are being reduced as a result of the end of the hostilities between the East and the West. The effort of the United Nations to increase attention to identifying the arms trade ought now to lead to efforts to control the arms trade and thus have a residual effect on developing nations of encouraging them to spend more on development through the savings effected by not purchasing arms.

RM: You can solve a problem with a vision, with an audacious new institution, or you can also solve a problem by throwing out thousands of little seeds. The United Nations does this in every possible direction. But when it comes to getting the decision of big powers to reduce their nuclear armaments, there is need for a bold vision to make real progress.

We have survived fifty years of the nuclear age. It is a miracle that we have survived. The longer nuclear weapons are maintained, the more the risks are that we cannot survive. That is my realistic assessment of the situation.

DR: Do you think there is any realistic hope of stopping the arms race throughout the South as long as the North maintains its vertical proliferation of nuclear weapons and continues to produce other weapons of mass destruction? In other words, unless there is a global ban on weapons of mass destruction, is there any hope of stopping their spread into the South?

RM: I wish the non-aligned countries would have the audacity to do what the others do not have the audacity to do. There is need for one or several great statesmen to take the leadership. On the other hand, one can do many good little things. At the University for Peace, we encourage developing countries to demilitarize themselves, following the example of Costa Rica. Panama has already done so. There are fourteen small countries in the world which are already demilitarized. Politicians are discovering that the only country in Central America where people have a good life and have no guerrillas and terrorism is Costa Rica. The military academy of El Salvador came for two weeks to find out how Costa Rica was able to live in a demilitarized way. We want to show that it is possible to have a security system under the Organization of American States. I would like to see a group of demilitarized countries created at the U.N. to induce other developing countries to get out of arms races and use their money for the welfare of their people.

DR: I want my own country to pursue a policy of demilitarization as a contribution to the abolition of war as a means of conflict resolution. But there is little political or public support for this idea. We have not yet, despite the end of the Cold War, got rid of the idea that militarism is necessary in order to resolve conflict. We do not put our faith or our trust in other instruments than war. We saw that instantly with the invasion of Kuwait. Conflict resolution was rejected in favour of a military buildup and a prosecution of war. We have not got militarism out of our heads, and consequently that is why we still have the sickness of violence infecting us and why that itself is an impediment to the deceleration of nuclear weapons to zero.

RM: The *Agenda for Peace* of the secretary-general, was considered to be great progress. It was great progress because, in addition to peacekeeping, it pointed out that we should also be active in the work of prevention and peacebuilding. On prevention, I would have liked the United Nations to create what NATO has, namely a NATO war room, but this would be a United Nations "Peace Room" on the thirty-ninth floor, where we would get information on every potential danger in the world. I would like to see a telecommunications system between all heads of state in their offices and their homes to be in direct contact, instead of listening to their diplomats who often complicate things to render themselves important and indispensable.

I'm in favor of the total abolition of the military planet-wide and to transform them from the top to the bottom into peacemakers and violence preventors, merging them with police forces who would also be renamed peace agents. The *Agenda for Peace* is already overtaken by something much wider. We must cope with the problem of violence at all levels: violence between nations, violence between races, violence between ethnic groups, violence between religions, violence in the cities, violence in the family, violence everywhere. If we came up with a new theory of nonviolence in the world and with methods to prevent it, then violence between nations would be seen as unethical from the beginning. I would deny a nation or group the right to use violence to solve a problem.

DR: The secretary-general, in outlining peacemaking as one of his four agenda items, raises the question of military intervention under Article 42. When the preventive diplomacy methods that he advocates fail, when the global watch system has indicated hostilities are about to break out, and when there is a legal reason to intervene because of a breakdown of law and order or the violations of human rights, the secretary-general is in favor of peacemaking defined as military action taken by forces operating under United Nations command. This is conflict resolution through military means. I want to know, in the light of what you have just said, whether or not you agree with that—whether this peacemaking role, in addition to peacekeeping, is justifiable under the United Nations Charter and in the wisdom of fifty years' experience.

RM: Yes, with one correction. They should not be called military, they should not be called forces, they should be peace protectors and servants.

DR: But they are going to fight, Robert.

RM: They don't have to fight. They should not have tanks and airplanes, but only temporarily numbing means. In the vision of a non-violent world, they should not look like militaries. I am glad that already they are called peace-protecting forces. That is progress. The military have undergone changes too. They do not function so much for war and aggression anymore, except in rare cases. They are not called ministries of war anymore, they are called ministries of defense or security. Nations, on the whole, are resolved to stay within their borders. We need to have peace-protecting forces, not military forces. Militarism is a barbarian, outdated system which is going to disappear anyway.

DR: War is a barbarian system of . . .

RM: Absolutely.

DR: resolving conflict . . .

RM: Exactly.

DR: We are beginning to learn that, but it has not yet seeped into public consciousness, at least at the public policy level. It is sweeping horizontally through the world. There is a resistance to war, a recognized horror to war. Nobody sings anymore about troops going off to war, as they did in my own childhood. That being said, there is still a public recognition that war is inevitable because the alternative instruments are not understood or trusted. Here is the secretary-general of the U. N., through the *Agenda for Peace,* trying to prevent hostilities but, when the prevention is insufficient, favouring a military intervention. The very debate that the world is now having about the proper uses of intervention—Bosnia, and Somalia being cases in point—and where the U.N. has not been successful, scares people about the United Nations. They don't realize that what needs to be done is to strengthen the U.N.'s system for peacemaking and peacekeeping to obviate the recourse to war. I want to make some progress in developing a greater confidence in the United Nations, but it is the major powers that prevent the U. N. from resolving conflict at early stages. You can't get political support for action at early stages. It's only after the explosion takes place that reactive forces then are employed.

RM: Many things can be done. The first is direct person-to-person diplomacy between heads of states, so that the underlings can no longer play their games. I remember saying that to the secretary-general in the case of a conflict which could have become another Middle East. The only solution was pick up the phone and tell the two leaders to solve the problem quickly between themselves. And the two leaders listened to him, met, and solved the problem.

Another factor is that the military are getting worried. They don't know what their future will be. The Honduran army informed us that they would be ready to plant trees all over Honduras in order not to lose their jobs. Nicaragua has reduced its military by 17,000 men, and Sweden has financed their conversion to environmental jobs. Many countries allow alternative service for young people. In Spain, a large percentage of youth work for the Red Cross instead of military service. This is what the fiftieth anniversary is all about: have a philosophy of life, have a love for this planet and all humans, have respect for the evolution in which we are involved. The whole world should join in this new approach and effort. Opponents speak about duplication in the United Nations. My God, if one would sit down and calculate the duplication of wasted military resources between 170 militarized nations, one would get sick . . .

DR: It's shocking.

RM: That is the revolution needed for successfully moving towards the year 2000. We have to use these last five years of the twentieth century to get leaders to understand they have to elevate, to transcend themselves. They have to understand that this is a cosmological, evolutionary process of paramount importance. They can do it. Why don't they try? They did it with the environment. There's now a concern for the earth that had not existed before.

DR: One of the most important sub-passages in the section on peace speaks of preventive action and diplomacy to be given a higher priority in the list of actions by the international community. Surely, much of what we have been saying here about peace points to the need for the abolition of war in coincidence with the abolition of nuclear weapons. This requires the development of instrumentalities for conflict resolution with a stronger legal and financial basis. This ought to be highlighted in the fiftieth anniversary declaration. That's one very distinct contribution that is not pie-in-the-sky as some people would say about the abolition of nuclear weapons. Preventive diplomacy can save lives immediately. What do you think should be the essence of preventive diplomacy written into the fiftieth anniversary declaration?

RM: I would start at even an earlier stage than preventive diplomacy and look at the causes of violence. We need a whole theory on violence in the world. I have recommended a world conference on non-violence to take the whole subject of why is there violence from the nation state down to the individual. When people are hungry in the streets, they become violent. There are reports that most of the violence among the adults and youth is due to television and not to the violent character of the family. We need an education and media to make all humans nonviolent beings. We must use the opportunity of the millennium to bring this to the forefront. U Thant would have been the ideal secretary-general for this because, for him, violence was the ultimate insult to life. I remember he said to me once: "Robert, you Westerners see violence in terms of physical violence, verbal violence, television violence, but you have never thought of what the real cause of violence is, the violence in your own mind."

DR: I believe that a new understanding of nonviolence in the post-Cold War era as we approach the millennium would be the real peace dividend. In order to move towards a better world, we must move towards a nonviolent world.

CHAPTER 3

Equality: Toward a New Philosophy

RM: Rather than the ideal of equality, it is inequalities that are highlighted nowadays.

What was nonequality in the question of apartheid? One race was treated inferiorally and this problem had to be dealt with. The United Nations has taken up very forcefully the lack of equality between males and females; a fourth World Conference on Women will deal with this issue in Beijing. Another enormous field of inequality, which the United Nations constantly deals with, is the lack of equality between the poor and the rich, both between countries and also inside countries, as the World Social Summit illustrates. The inequality of the handicapped has also been taken up by the U.N.. The handicapped had very few rights and very little recognition. Thanks to the U.N. International Year of the Handicapped, a handicapped person is considered as an equal human being for which nations have to care, provide facilities, transportation, etc. Other fields of inequality are abandoned human beings, especially children, and refugees. If you go to camps of refugees, you cannot say that these people are on an equal footing with the rest of the population. They are diminished, even in freedom of movement, by their status of refugee.

It would be worthwhile to have a science of equality, a science of peace, a science of justice, followed by a strategy to deal with various inequalities. We also need methodologies of how to solve these problems. And, finally, inspection. After the United Nations has said that the equality of women and males should take place, how do you monitor this nationally and internationally? Just as we have a University for Peace, which forces us to reflect on and develop a science, a strategy, and a methodology of peace, as the military do for war or defense, there should be a United Nations university on equality of human beings. That could be a promising project.

DR: At the outset, one would think this an easy element to handle in a consensus declaration, given the fame of the Universal Declaration of Human Rights and the two covenants on civil and political rights and economic and social rights. The basis for universal human rights has been particularly strengthened by the 1993 Vienna Declaration on Human Rights. But as I have been reflecting on this, I think that equality is perhaps the most difficult of all the elements. We do not yet have an understanding of equality in the world.

Of course, we are not all equal in the world. Some people are born with high intelligence and some are born with low intelligence. Some are born with handicaps, some are born without handicaps. There is a distinction between equality and sameness.

I interpret the word equality to mean equitability. There is a distinct lack of equitability, shown most dramatically in the split between the North and the South. The population of the world will reach 8.2 billion or so in the next twenty years; approximately 7 billion will live in the South and 1 billion in the North. There is a worsening ecosphere stress factor: approximately one-fifth of the world in the North has access to and control over three-quarters of the capital and technology and resources of the world while four-fifths living in the South have access to only one-quarter of the capital and technology.

This leads to the ultimate question the world has to face as to the carrying capacity of the planet, given the exploitation that persists at the hands of the minority. As a minority, we are in this planetary boat resisting the importunities of those who are clamouring to get into the boat and looking for a common means of managing the planet. It is the determination of the strong to maintain their position by whatever means necessary, whether military or financial or political, that is the basis of the systemic inequality in the world.

The North resists even a dialogue on global economic negotiations to take in such questions as resources and raw materials and trade and finances so that the South would have equitable access to these means of ensuring the fulfillment of basic human needs on a universal basis. This perpetuates great divisiveness in the world. In looking to the U.N. declaration for the fiftieth anniversary dealing with equality, I wonder what they are going to say beyond the opening words: "The Charter reaffirms our faith in the dignity and worth of the human person, in the equal rights of men and women and of nations large and small." Just because we recognize human rights through declarations, how is that going to change human conduct?

RM: The three short lines on equality are indeed sparse. You can see that the drafters are a little bit at a loss and that this is one of the thorniest issues because people are unequal in their capacities and also the way they start their lives. It makes quite a difference to be born in a rich, influential family or in a poor, humble one. Nevertheless, it is a good start. Trying to reduce inequalities and not let them continue or increase in all human categories, be it women, indigenous people, minorities, small states, big states, the poor and the rich, cannot be ignored by the United Nations on a world scale.

In this context, we should also look at the recent claim for privatization, which is not just about business and economics. Much public service for the poor in the countries is being ruthlessly destroyed in the name of privatization. Private liberty and values are also limited by a systematic programming by business, advertising, and the media. In each country on earth there should be a ministry for consumer protection and private liberty. And a U.N. agency should be created with the same name for the world as a whole.

DR: We are accustomed to measuring success in terms of the GNP, the gross national product. This is the reason why the *Human Development Report*, which gives a new index of measuring true human security, is a valuable instrument.[1] The accent in the post–Cold War era on the building of the market and the conjoining of the market to democracy, as if the two were one, is a further manifestation of why the equality section of the elements document is so brief. To extend it is to get into areas of great controversy.

If we are moving to the concept of common security, in which nations are supposed to cooperate with one another rather

---

1. United Nations Development Program, *Human Development Report* (New York: Oxford University Press, 1994).

than confront one another in pursuing security, then common security on a nation-state level does focus on the need for systemic change in the way nations operate. The old balance of power system that has prevailed for the better part of three hundred years, in which the strong dominated the weak and used muscle, a.k.a. military and now nuclear arms, to effect their domination, is an impediment to common security. So a systemic change is required in the relationships between states in order to have common security. Before we get to a systemic change at the nation-state level, we need a much greater understanding of the human aspect of our relationships.

My contention here is that we have not yet begun to understand the full meaning of human rights, despite their proclamation in lovely, rhetorical ways. I don't mean to be dismissive of the need for declarations and the need for articulating a concern. But when it comes down to it, we are tolerating a violence against people, we are tolerating an intrusion of human rights every day. It's violence to have forty thousand children dying daily because of waterborne diseases and malnutrition and easily controllable things. It's violence against our planet to have the ozone layer depleted by industrial states, which put industrial development before the good of the environment. It is certainly violence against me personally to be subjected to the effects of weapons of mass destruction having the power to decimate huge areas of the world. The need for a new understanding of the roots of violence in the post–Cold War era is perhaps seen most clearly in this concept of equality. How we are to have equitability built into human and thus state relations is a huge challenge as we enter the new millennium.

RM: I would add one further subject of concern, namely the equality between small businesses and gigantic businesses. I give you the example of Costa Rican restaurants, which used to serve a large variety of natural fruit juices, made locally. Now this small industry has been practically killed by Coca Cola and other soft drink manufacturers. Advertising is programming the people. And if you write a letter of complaint, the newspapers will not publish it because they get advertising money from these firms. Here you have the example of a huge, world-wide, almost monopoly of soft drinks, which is killing the little businesses and enterprises in the developing countries. Coca Cola will tell you, oh, but we are a private business and all you have to do is buy a share in Coca Cola and then you are a co-owner of the firm. Yes, but the co-owners of Coca Cola are in the United States and the West, not in Costa Rica. Few people here even know what a share is. They do not have the resources to buy any.

The inequality between gigantic business and small business should be stressed. Now in Colombia they have a new policy of financially supporting micro enterprises because the government has found that with one thousand dollars of investment in a small local business, they will get one person employed, whereas to create one job in a big enterprise, you have to put in twenty thousand dollars of capital. I am very pleased to learn that the World Bank, along with the Inter-American Bank, is going to give loans to small businesses.

DR: One of the reasons that the New International Economic Order, advanced through United Nations auspices in the mid-seventies, foundered was because of this very resistance to equality or to equitability. The basis of the South's claim was that there was a right to development for every human being. That means you have a right to access those goods and instruments necessary for the extension of basic human needs. This has been resisted by the North through the years because of what they perceive as its consequences: a sharing of resources rather than exploitation. If you want a current example of this, look only at the common heritage of the seas. One of the reasons the Law of the Sea has been so watered down is because major states have refused to recognize that the minerals, constituting a vast amount of wealth in the common areas of the oceans, should be shared. The sharing provisions of the Law of the Sea as it was originally written have now been changed to allow the major states with high technology to go in and get that money and consequently become even richer. The concepts of sharing and of stewardship of the planet that are so necessary in order to have a common security are still a long way off.

RM: This is why I recommended the creation of a World Commission for the Seas and Oceans to continue the battle. And I hope that one will be created for the aboliton of nuclear weapons. We are living on a planet where everything now has to be seen from a global point of view. We know the planet, we have a total picture of it. All these issues come to the fore in the United Nations. It is the role of the United Nations to advance all ethical and moral issues. After long years of opposition, some begin to be solved. Take labor conflicts. In the last century and at the beginning of this century, the main form of violence on the planet was labor violence. It even led to Communism. The International Labor Organization was created in 1919 with employers, employees, and government representatives. Today, labor violence is practically nil, thanks to the agreements and conflict resolution techniques worked out in the ILO.

Institutions can play an enormous role in bringing about more equality. Proper taxation is a foremost one. I would recommend that the former Fiscal Commission of the U.N. Economic and Social Council, for which I worked at the beginning of my U.N. career, be reestablished. For women, national legislation for equality is greatly advanced. When I married, my wife, who was from Chile, was not allowed to go to university by her family! There was not a single woman doctor of law in Chile, nor a woman diplomat. Today in Chile, women have equal rights, even sometimes more rights than men. Look at apartheid. Everybody thought that there would be no solution to apartheid. The race equality is not yet what it should be, but the U.N. has advanced the equitability of those formerly deemed unequal. Philosophy in practice is one of the trademarks of the United Nations.

DR: It is evident that one of the great successes of the United Nations in advancing the concept of equality is in the field of women's rights. The great conferences that have been held, particularly "The Nairobi Forward-Looking Strategies for the Advancement of Woman," have empowered women. I noticed that in your novel, *First Lady of the World*, you created a woman as the first female secretary-general of the United Nations.[2] I thought that was an effort on your part to make a statement that you believe the goals of peace and security and the ending of war—the humanization of the world—would be advanced by women being at the centers of influence. Did I read your mind right in setting the novel in those terms?

RM: Yes. The feminine touch has not been allowed to play its proper role. No mother on earth considers that it would be good for her son to be killed in a war. We have a beautiful inscription here on the monument at the University for Peace: "Happy the Costa Rican mother who when she gives birth to a son knows that he will never be a soldier." Some day all mothers on earth should be able to say that.

----

2. Robert Muller, *First Lady of the World* (Anacortes, Wash.: World Happiness and Cooperation, 1991).

When you look at the representation of women in the decision-making places, it is not acceptable that since the creation of the United States, there has never been a woman president. It is not normal that we should end this century with not a single woman having become secretary-general of the United Nations. At least, there are now three or four more women under secretaries-general and assistant secretaries-general. My novel will definitely have an impact. I wrote it in memory of my deceased wife who was one of the great advocates of women's rights at the U.N.

DR: One wants to hope that the nurturing characteristics of women could be applied to the political realm. I don't want to make too much of a point of this, but, while agreeing generally with that concept, and certainly wanting to see more equitable representation of the genders in policy-making positions in the world, I have noted that there are many women in a position of influence who still play the male power game. Is that because they are afraid of being written off by their male co-workers? Or maybe there isn't that much biological difference, after all. I think that this is a whole subject all by itself. I hope women would recognize that, as equitable access to power gradually comes about, they can only really fulfill their destiny by advancing agendas leading to greater true human security.

RM: Perhaps women who come into power become iron women because they are scared they will lose the next election or will be criticized for not having the strength of men. But I don't think that they are genetically prone to the same attitude as man. Man in the primeval society had to fight to get food and the female's role was to protect the children. The fights have changed in character, but are not as violent as they were in the past. I think that women should have a greater role. It makes quite a difference when a child is born from your own flesh. You don't want to see it killed or to kill others. If more women were in favor, we could obtain in the U.N. a new fundamental human right which I advocate relentlessly: the right not to kill and not to be killed, not even in the name of a nation.

DR: The equality section also speaks about indigenous peoples. We have only recently come to recognize the inherent qualities of indigenous peoples, that the atrocities committed against them by so-called civilized people, along with the sublimation of inherent cultural and ethnic values in indigenous peoples, is one of the great outrages of this closing millennium. The resistance against the celebration of the 500th anniversary of Columbus' discovery of America because of what was done to the native peoples of the Americas is but one illustration of why this subject needs far more attention. The problems that obtain in many indigenous societies today—alcoholism and drugs and all these other problems stemming from an inability to access systems that have been overlaid on them by the "white man"—are still very much with us.

RM: One of the main contributions of the indigenous people and also one of our main interests in getting closer to them is that this subject is connected to the environmental issue. Indigenous people still have a feeling for the right relations with Mother Earth and with nature, which we have lost. We can learn much philosophy from them. For example, the Iroquois ruled never to take a decision without thinking of the effects on the seventh generation. Who today thinks even of the next generation? There is much wisdom in indigenous people, who have not lost contact with Mother Earth and with their wise cosmologies. By the way, on the occasion of the International Year of the Family, I learned something very important from the Maya Indians. A husband

and wife have an incredibly long lineal ascendance on both sides. In other words, the family is the result of the evolution of thousands of ancestors, and it produces children who will be at the origin of thousands of descendants of society, not the individual. So, the family is at the center because it is the family that procreates, it is the union of two streams of evolution.

DR: The document also speaks of minorities as needing a higher priority on future agendas. When I think about minorities, it reminds me of the great paradox that is taking place in the world today. At the very moment that globalization is sweeping the world and all the systems—finance, security, environment and trade and so on—are coming together in a planetary sense, there is an outbreak of minority rights and intense conflict in many regions. Violence accompanies this self determination. The need to advance minority rights without fanning the fires of nationalism is crashing against the need for continued globalization of the world. The world is getting bigger and smaller at the same time. That's what I mean by a paradox. And I wonder how the rights of minorities through the U.N. declaration can be advanced in a manner that is harmonious with globalization.

RM: Every species has things which are common characteristics, but there are not two trees on earth, even of the same species, likely to be the same. With humans, it is exactly the same. The whole planet is a united system, an interdependent system. The whole biosphere, the little layer of life which surrounds our planet, is only a few miles thick. In this thin sphere-membrane of life called the biosphere, everything is interdependent and relates to every other. The main characteristic of the planet is infinite biodiversity. At the same time, we must be respectful of the totality of the biosphere. This is one reason why I no longer believe so much in humans on the one side and the environment on the other side. Unity in diversity within an infinity of harmonious groupings is the evolutionary law we must obey.

DR: It seems to me that the quest for minority rights clashes with the societal responsibilities to advance in a unified way the global pattern that has now emerged in the technological age. Since the end of the Cold War, this almost desperate quest to achieve a new status for minorities is impeding the globalization agenda for common security.

RM: We have the two phenomena. On the one hand we have the growth of geographic communities, like the European community and a dozen other regional communities. Globalization progresses. At the same time, diversity progresses too, down to the individual and the liberty of associating with other people. A family has the right to be a family. You do not want to be bossed around by the neighbours, you do not want to have the state intervene in your bedroom, you have a unit which makes a lot of sense. If you have people who gather together around a certain language, which they have inherited from the past, along with certain customs and physical features, they have a right to associate too, but not to assert themselves over others. The whole question of unity in diversity is at stake. Here our political philosophy for the planet is not yet what it should be. We have to think this out—from the global to the local and the individual. What will be a normal, peaceful, harmonious human society at all levels?

Religions have an important role to play, in humility and love, in fostering ethnic peace. If I were the secretary-general, one of the first things I would do is to establish an office in the United Nations for peace-making between ethnic and religious groups.

Coming from a region of France and Europe called Alsace-Lorraine, I have a good example of unity in diversity: we have our local language, our local customs and traditions, our beautifully preserved centuries-old villages, our special famous cooking, but it would not occur to us to ask for independence or autonomy. It is much easier to live within the greater area of France and now, entire Europe. We have not submitted to France or Germany, we have annexed both to a larger European Union where we find employment and a role. You will find Alsace-Lorrainers in many international organizations. We are bilingual from birth. And there are thousands of tourists who come to visit our extraordinary region. Well, the whole world should look like that, not a boring, uniform world, but a world of infinite biodiversity and including human, cultural biodiversity.

DR: A place where the global and the individual come together in a sphere where you would think there could be consensus is the area of children. The 1990 Summit on Children produced a great declaration and a convention affirming the rights of the child. That was a considerable accomplishment of the U.N. in advancing human rights in the framework of equality. What we now see is the reluctance of nation-states to follow their own rhetoric with budgetary priorities. The funding that was spoken of to implement the rights of the child quickly fell apart at the very time when the Gulf War was getting started, overnight some $60 billion was found by the cooperating nations in the prosecution of the Gulf War. But money was impossible to find to implement that which had already been decided in the advancement of children's rights, including immunization and health and education. This points once more to the fundamental challenge we are still facing. A new stage in history has arrived, in which we have the knowledge, the brains to solve our problems and to advance children as a unifying element whatever the culture or religion. But we do not yet give, through the budgetary priorities of nation-states, the attention to fulfilling those elementary needs—which is why we are still left, as we enter the new millennium, with the outrageous statistics of the deaths from malnutrition and suffering of children.

RM: Well, I could point out that it is the same with peace and war. Trillions are spent on the military and armaments, but the first Peace University on this planet is left without practically any resources. Our priorities on this planet need serious revision. We are in need of a world budget.

The basic problem we have on the eve of the next millennium is the need for a new, right philosophy. Philosophy is the art of living, the way of living. We have not tried to find a common philosophy for human life, its meaning, reproduction, and behaviour on earth. If your philosophy is wrong, then your priorities are wrong. And if your priorities are wrong, your resources are maldistributed. We have a maldistribution and misallocation of resources on a colossal scale because priorities are not in conformity with a common philosophy. The United Nations is becoming a philosophical organization, not because it has this as its objective, but because of increasing demand. It does this progressively by sorting out the problems. Children are precious because they are the new units of evolution. You have to educate them to pursue cosmological evolution.

The U.N. has also looked at the elderly. It took us a long time until we got the first World Conference on Aging. We will have an International Year of the Elderly. They have wisdom, they have something to contribute, they are a vital link with the new generation.

That we have problems, that we make mistakes, that we are too slow, reluctant, and hesitant is a fact, but let us never forget that this is the first time in the entire human history that we are attempting to solve problems on a world scale. Speaking about the global and the individual or the local, my dream is that every human being would be educated in such a way that he or she would be both global and simultaneously local, both universal and very individual. As William Blake once said: "To see the beauty of the universe and the stars and to see it in a flower." The same individual can look at the blue sky and say how marvelous this is, where does it end, where is the infinity of this universe—and then see a child or another human being or one of the incredible creations of nature. As humans, we are enhanced by the total universe both in its infinity and in its smallness. But we are still in a global kindergarten of proper planetary management, of good behavior, peace, philosophy, and global and individual fulfillment.

CHAPTER 4

Justice: Universal Enforcement Needed

RM: I note the great volume of U.N. material on peace and development. There is less on equality and justice. Frankly, the United Nations has not dared to get to the bottom of what equality is and what justice is. There is some kind of psychological reservation or political obstacle. Examining the days proclaimed by the United Nations, there are half a dozen on development, and quite a few on peace. There are some on human rights, but when you come to justice, you don't find much. Institutionally in the U.N. itself, there is no central department that looks at equality or justice in their totality.

Just as we first see inequality, we first see injustice and note the crassest injustices. But we should consider what is just for us as human beings. That leads to human rights. What is the instrument of justice that will guarantee that my human rights are preserved? You come to the conclusion that the concept of justice in reality and instrumentalities of justice in the United Nations systems are mostly justice in terms of international relations. What is just and what is unjust from the point of view of a nation? This is why there are hundreds of agreements and many efforts to promote all kinds of efforts of tolerance.

What has come to the fore recently is justice for the individual. What is justice for an entity, for an ethnic group, for a religion, for a municipality, for a corporation? What is justice from their point of view? For the whole series of entities from the individual and the family to the human community? We now also speak of justice for the earth. What is just and what is unjust in our treatment of the earth? Justice is still mainly a product of national sovereignty. Countries are sovereign and as sovereign entities seek some kind of justice among themselves. Unfortunately, there is nothing on the world level to ensure justice toward an individual. Certain countries have declared in advance that the judgments of the International Court of Justice will not be applicable to them. The World Court has no enforcement capacity. A strange justice indeed!

DR: I want to begin by emphasizing one of the last words you just used, the word "enforcement." I am torn on this issue of justice. I recognize that a great deal has been developed under the auspices of the United Nations to foster international law. There are hundreds of international treaties and, increasingly, multilateral treaties have more signatures affixed to them. There is a widening of the understanding of the need for international law. Indeed, we are living in the decade for international law in the 1990s. But I also recognize that the world is still at a primitive state given the need for enforceable law to manage the planet.

Look, would you live in a community where your two neighbours on either side fill their houses with ammunition, dynamite, and train their guns at each other right past your front window? Of course, you wouldn't, and you don't have to because in virtually every society there is local law to prevent desperadoes or outlaws from stocking their houses at your peril. And yet, globally speaking, that is exactly how we have lived all through the Cold War. As a Canadian, in that piece of planetary real estate situated between the United States and the Soviet Union, both of whom mounted enormous arsenals of nuclear weapons trained at one another to destroy their cities, it would be impossible for Canada to escape the consequences of any such war. And I was powerless to invoke law to prevent that occurrence. I had to wait until the Cold War ended, for reasons that have to do with perhaps a synergy of energy of peoples rather than the application of law.

So for me, in being torn between these two views, I have to recognize that the evolution of our planet brings us to a stage where my neighbor is not just the person with whom I am in geographical proximity, but my neighbor is the person on the other side of the world. Technology has made me aware of that and also enabled me to communicate and to reach that person. It follows for me that just as I expect justice for myself and justice for my neighbor, I have to expect justice for people wherever they are. This brings us to the point that you were making of the inherent right to justice that people have wherever they are.

Now what is justice? The great debate revolves around this question. That is why we find so little or relatively little material in the U.N. on justice and equality whereas in development and peace there is a great deal of material and activity. Even in the elements for the declaration for the fiftieth anniversary, there are only a few lines dealing with the subject of justice. I feel that they want to pay more than lip service to it, but they cannot deal with it in a more substantive way until they recognize the equality of all individuals and the need therein for protective measures in law. That law which we observe at the domestic level has to be applied at the international level, and what is getting in the way of that is the whole concept—I would even say the boogie man—of nationalist sovereignty.

RM: You are right. But there are a few hopeful signs which have surfaced in the last few years, indicating there will be a change in the future.

There is a Court of Human Rights for Latin America established here in Costa Rica where the judgments of the courts are enforceable. This is new, but it's only enforceable between states; an individual cannot have a private lawsuit and then get a compensation from the government from that court.

In Europe, an enormous jump has been made with the creation of the European Union because today there is a European court of justice where an individual can sue his or her government, seeking the rights which have been given to individuals under the European Union, which include the right to cross the border to do business, to establish oneself in any country of the European Union. If this right is impeded, the individual can go to the court and the court will force the government to pay an indemnity to repair the injustice to the individual. This is enormous, because for the first time, an individual can go to a supranational court and get his own government condemned.

Another forward step is the development of what one could call international courts of criminal justice. We had the Nuremberg trials against the Nazi leaders and torturers of World War II, which was unique. This was really a world tribunal to condemn people who had created injustices like the Holocaust on a massive scale. There recently emerged supranational criminal courts of justice for similar acts in Bosnia and other places.

It is also interesting to note that, under the national sovereignty system, a dictator can appear at the United Nations. Because he represents his government, how he got to power is not even challenged. There is now more and more talk of challenging dictatorships and making orderly representation at the U.N. dependent on a true democracy.

DR: In these discussions, we are trying not to engage in lamentation, although as one looks around the world, there is a fair amount to lament. What occupies our attention here is trying to find a vision for the future: to help people summon up the strengths and resources that are needed for change.

You have rightly pointed to the emergence of the concept of world tribunals against those who perpetrate criminal acts of war or violence on massive scales. I would call these the spectacular cases. The U.N. is now struggling to get developed or regularized, a world tribunal. What I am concerned about is the justice that is demanded by those who suffer silently. The forty thousand children who die every day from malnutrition and waterborne diseases have their claim for justice too, but there is no world tribunal and world court for them. I suppose this is because human beings caught up in the crises that dominate the headlines sweep by this and merely apply some concepts of charity and even some concepts of social justice. But we need legal justice for those so victimized. This means a world system of law. But the opponents of true legal justice see what they would call the specter of world government. It is because they oppose allowing an international body to apply the concepts of law with the penalties for conviction that they resist enlarged justice.

Finally, it seems to me, that as we talk about common security and the integral rights of individuals, there is a logical extension of this that requires a universal law, maintained by a universal

authority that is itself responsible internationally to some authority. Who is this authority? The closest is the Security Council of
the United Nations, which itself is not representative of the modern world. Moreover, the powerful nation-states maintain veto
power to stop that which they do not like. I don't want to mix too
many areas of activity into this general subject of justice. I'm only
trying to indicate that I believe the development of enforceable
world law to establish and maintain the conditions for human
security based on disarmament and development and environmental protection is denied us by the forces of the strong and the
powerful who see their power threatened.

RM: I want to make a few proposals of what could be done by
the United Nations. For example, there is no U.N. body to deal
with justice or with equality. Such a body could deal with peace
and development under the principle of justice. We could have
an International Year of Justice. There could also be an International Year of Equality in order to upgrade these moral, philosophical concepts.

Although world government is opposed by those in power,
how would the opponents of a federal system or a better world
system feel if George Washington had not had the courage to put
order among the American states, which hated and even fought
one other. I look up to the United States, which had the courage
to create a federal system for itself, to have the audacity to propose the same or a similar system for the entire world.

Why not have the courage to look into a new world order
which would comprise a world supreme court to protect individuals everywhere? There could be a parliamentary assembly of the
U.N. to speak for the voiceless, such as the homeless and abandoned children. The world is moving in this direction whether
the big powers like it or not. The sooner we create these new

institutions, the better our chance of saving the planet and of producing a happier humanity. This must be said during the fiftieth anniversary of the U.N. Even if it cannot be solved in a few months, a proper system of global government should be made a permanent, prominent item on the U.N. agenda.

DR: I found it interesting that the U.N. committee preparing the document for the fiftieth anniversary state that, recognizing the progress that has been made, we must give special attention to finding justice in the fields of information, communication, finance, trade and investment. It is notable that they singled out information and communication. Consider the need to apply the concept of justice to information and communication. Are people today deprived of the correct information on which to make the decisions of their life? Are they deprived of sufficient information?

The war in Somalia became important because CNN was there. There are lots of wars going on in Africa, but nobody hears anything about them because the media are not there. That's just by way of illustration that the search, as UNESCO tried, for a new world information order was fought to the death by the powerful interests of the North that distorted the issue by saying this was going to be censorship of information and so on. In fact, there is a censorship of information now going on. When the Gulf War was taking place, professional survey organizations established the fact that the major networks, by huge ratios, carried the opinions of people who were prowar and very seldom carried opinions of people who were opposed to the war. The development of a consciousness of stewardship and sharing needs to be applied to information and communication. I take heart in the fact that in the fiftieth anniversary document they are at least pointing to, even if by indirection and subtlety, this very real problem of information and communication.

RM: This raises another question. Within a country like the United States, there is an antitrust law. Corporations are not allowed to have a monopoly. But they can get a monopoly worldwide. The United Nations has never been authorized to devise a system to protect the weak and to prevent the monopoly of great enterprises. In other words, there are many multinational corporations which can do around the world what they cannot do at home. And the national government looks with pleasure on these multinational corporations bringing in money to their country. Most of the governments have become servants, not of the public, but of the multinational corporations, which have globalized themselves. Concerning UNESCO, there is little doubt that advancing a new world information order led the United States to leave UNESCO, not the perennial accusation of bureacracy and maladministration.

DR: The document also points to finance, trade, and investment as areas requiring attention in the subject of justice. What does this tell us? What about the role of the World Bank and the International Monetary Fund as the main financial instruments? What about the role of the World Trade Organization? Are these mega-international instruments working to apply justice or are they working to apply the economic decisions made by the major states that established them? This is certainly a question that many people challenge today, and I again take heart when I see the finance, trade, and investment questions related to justice in the U.N. document.

RM: This is one of the advantages of holding the U.N. anniversary. Certain things which are not correct and have to be corrected can be pointed out. I hope that out of this declaration there will be new moves in the United Nations to change certain philosophies based on the past. The Bank and the Fund were founded on the premise that the bigger the company, the larger the economies of scale, the better for the people. That was the theory. Give the money to the very big ones because there will be returns from them and economic efficiency, which the small firms are incapable of. This has to be challenged because we have now unprecedented unemployment, which the big corporations have not been able to prevent. We need to look at the whole concept of employment and offer an economy which is much more diversified and which protects the individual and does not help the big corporation to become bigger and bigger. Even the Bank is beginning to recognize this and says that from now on it will give loans to little agriculturists or little businesses.

DR: When the document uses the words ... "make wider use of the international judicial system," is this a code for trying to say enforcement or a path to enforcement? How much longer can the World Court be denied a mandatory compliance? Are we not on a path that will demand that the credibility of the World Court be enhanced by giving it the enforcement powers that law requires? It seems to me to be a logical progression. The wider use of the international judicial system for the settlement of disputes can itself be part of the preventive diplomacy concept.

RM: Here, I want to return to the fact that the world is on the eve of a new millennium. The fiftieth anniversary of the U.N. is not so much to look at the past but to look audaciously at the future and make recommendations as to how we could succeed better. In order to bring to light certain basic deficiencies in the world system or in world relations, we must have the courage to think big. For example, in our discussion on peace, we have come to the conclusion that today the problem is far beyond peace between nations. It is peace between ethnic groups, between religions, it is peace in the family, it is peace in the streets, and that we ought to have a world conference on violence at all levels. In the field of justice, we also need a big push. Why not hold a world conference on justice? We wouldn't even know at present what the agenda would be, but we could review every aspect of justice on the planet. Let's not limit this to international justice. Let us go to fundamental injustices. It would enlighten the minds of people and the governments as to what the United Nations is about.

DR: I think that there is a fear of the consequences of international justice. Not a fear in the U.N. itself but a fear in the major powers. In the colonial age, we exploited peoples because we thought we had a right to do it. Even in the past—thankfully the distant past—religion thought it had a right to pursue and prosecute wars. Today we understand we cannot occupy other lands as was done in the colonial period. That, I suppose, is a big step forward. But there is a fear that persists that if the elements of justice are to be fully applied universally, we in the North will have to adjust our way of life. Our way of life has been built on economic domination and exploitation, if no longer in the colonial sense, then certainly in the economic sense. We justify our way of life by saying that we are developing the overall engine of economic development in the world, and this is going to be good for the poor people. It is this concept of fear of justice that I think is a retarding element.

RM: What the nation-state does today is say to its people: if you do not vote for us and our policy you will not be protected. You have prosperity because we are here, because we take the necessary measures, we are your protectors. This is the problem. There are enormous pressures building up around the world that can turn against them. That can be very damaging to what they believe they can pursue for centuries to come.

What I find wonderful, after having spent so many years in the United Nations, is that at least we have a place where such questions can be raised. No stone can remain uncovered for long in the United Nations. The fiftieth anniversary is contributing to it. Who else will raise the question of world equality and world justice? No national institute would do this. The U. N., with its 185 countries, some of them victims of injustices, is a place where all this converges and where humanity is trying to find its way. I'm sure that, twenty years from now, the United Nations will have been as successful in solving internal, ethnic, and other conflicts as it has been in resolving international conflicts.

DR: I am attracted by your concept of the convergence of humanity at the U.N. We need to emphasize, as we try to have a vision of justice, that it is not the homogenization of the world we are seeking—as if everybody is going to become the same. Not at all. We want to pursue justice in its international dimensions to protect the differences so that peoples, religions, and cultures, and their own histories can be protected. It is accenting justice that will help us to solidify that. Let us take some satisfaction, if not yet supreme joy, in the gains that the United Nations is making in extending the hand of international justice.

RM: It is a pity that to this great concept they have not added the concept of freedom because that raises the question of freedom of association. To be part of a religion, to be part an ethnic group, to be part of any association raises the issue of freedom of the individual to seek like-minded people and to create new associations with new purposes. That is a fundamental component of human society. This is how biology works: by endless diversification and combinations and trying to find better means. Freedom should have been added to the four concepts.

CHAPTER 5

Development: The Human Person at the Center

DR: At the U.N., development has been called, "the most compelling task of the Organization." It certainly is. It would be a poor international system that did not produce human security for peoples of the world The problem of development cannot be viewed alone; it must be inserted into the overall framework of the document. We have to understand what is peace, what is equality, what is justice, before we come to development.

The problem of the sixties, when the world began to focus on development in the postcolonial era, was that we jumped in and thought development was the extension of mega-projects, and that would suffice to produce development. We have now learned that development is a complicated human process requiring education, health, and services at the local level to enable the human person to grow. We have learned that, even if we are not yet fully applying the lesson.

The issue of development starts with a consideration of who is the human person. It is the person that must be the object of the development process, not just the provision of infrastructures and various things at the top of the society. Permit me here a small anecdote to illustrate my own learning processes. Many years ago, I went to Bangladesh for the first time, and there I came across something known as the Earth Satellite Station, which was a magnificent structure sending signals back and forth to London for stock quotations and weather reports and so on. It doubtless had its own values. But surrounding the Earth Satellite Station was village after village of people who didn't have the most rudimentary elements of human life. And this anomaly, this contradiction, this paradox, this grotesque distortion of what development should be, was a lesson that I have carried through the years. For me, the purpose of development must include the concept of the whole person, and any process of growth that does not lead to the fulfillment of basic needs of food and shelter and education and health is a travesty of the idea of development.

RM: I have been involved in the work of the United Nations and development practically since the beginning. I will never forget the excitement prevailing in Lake Success, in the old war factory of Sperry-Rand, where the U. N. was established at the time, when the first technical assistance mission left for Haiti. The main concern in the United Nations was to alleviate poverty and misery in the world. This is why UNICEF was created to help the starving children, the World Health Organization created to prevent people from dying early from sickness, the FAO created to develop agriculture, UNESCO created to promote science, the arts, and education. We wanted the same advantages of western progress to reach people around the world. It was a fantastic story.

During that period, the International Finance Corporation, the International Development Association, and the World Food Program, channeling surpluses to the developing countries, were all instituted. This machinery created by the Economic and Social Council is one of the great pages of human history.

As we dealt with economic development, in our ignorance of the whole state of the planet, and of the functioning of the planet, we made a number of mistakes, and we continue to make mistakes. The most fundamental one was to run to the developing countries, to help them to save the children, without having a population policy to recommend to them. Until 1952, we didn't even know how many people lived on the planet! We woke up at the end of the sixties and discovered that there was a population explosion because children didn't die in the former large numbers and women continued to have six or seven children. Parents had traditionally large families in order to have at least two or three left at the end of their lives to take care of them and cultivate the land.

The whole problem of economic development could have been solved at that time when we had a world population of around two and a half billion people. Since then, we have become 5.7 billion. Today, when we look at the world situation, despite longevity having increased here and there, child mortality having diminished, illiteracy having diminished, the absolute figures are still colossal.

Here, in a nutshell, is an illustration given by the U.S. Peace Corps as a guide to introduce global education in the classroom. The 5.7 billion people of the planet are reduced to a village of 100 people: 50 are malnourished, 33 have no clean, safe drinking water, 70 are illiterate, and only one would have a college education. Out of the 100, 58 are Asian, 12 are African, 10 are Western European, 8 are Latin Americans, 5 are North Americans, and 1 is Australian or a New Zealander. That is the picture today.

Thankfully, an improvement has begun in containing population growth. In 1970, on the twenty-fifth anniversary of the U.N., the world population in the year 2000 was estimated to reach 7.3 billion people. The estimate is now down to 6.1 billion people. The population policies advocated by the U.N. have lead to the fact that 1.2 billion fewer people are born in these critical years of adjustment. The population problem continues to worsen, but at a slower rate. It might take until the year 2100 to get to a halt.

DR: Here is my, for once, highly optimistic view. I think the population problem is beaten. The problem is behind us. The spread of knowledge about and technology of populations is now effective—not perfect by any means, but certainly far more than it was ten and twenty years ago. The education of women, which is now a foremost characteristic of many national policies, is itself contributing to the solution of the population problem. I have seen this in recent tours through developing countries. The gross projections for populations that the UNFPA made some years ago are going to be revised.

However, when I say that the population problem is behind us, this is not to say that we don't have a terrible problem caused by the ecosphere stress factor, in which so few people retain control over so much of the world and so many of the world have access to so little. I do not mean for one second to diminish the intensity of that problem which continues. For me, the population problem is not just a problem of numbers, it is a problem of consumption in the North. It is a problem of people who have grown accustomed to the benefits of the exploitation of the resources of the world for the benefit of the strong. That is where the element of the population problem must be viewed.

The Cairo Conference, under the auspices of the U.N., established clearly the interrelationships between population, sustained economic growth and sustainable development. From yet another U.N. avenue, we see how the interrelated aspects of the human security issues must all be dealt with simultaneously. We cannot deal only with population, we cannot deal only with environment, we cannot deal just with development as if putting up some edifice or some structure is development. Development is an integrative aspect of the liberation of humanity.

RM: The problem of overconsumption, which was completely neglected until recently, is now coming strongly to the fore. With the environment, it was the same thing. Twenty-five years ago, there was not a single ministry of the environment. Today there are no ministries of consumption. Although the environment continues to deteriorate, it does so at a slower rate. Thanks to the U.N., the population and environment problems are in the process of being solved.

Now about overconsumption, here is an interesting statistic. At the end of his or her life, the average person in the developing country leaves behind 150 times his or her weight in solid waste. The average American leaves behind a mountain of waste 4,000 times his or her own weight! Information of this kind is being published by the World Commission on Population and Quality of Life in Paris.

Beyond the question of overconsumption and population, we come to the question of happiness, of the meaning of life. In spite of the two-fold increase in per capita spending for personal consumption, the number of U.S. citizens describing themselves as very happy is no larger than it was in 1957. It has fluctuated around the one-third mark ever since. Moreover, today you have junk from the rich countries penetrating the developing countries. When smoking was prohibited in some rich countries, advertisement for and the marketing of cigarettes were stepped up in the South. This is why I have been clamouring for a World Conference on Marketing and Advertising.

DR: You and I both deal with mountains of statistics. I will only refer to one statistic. It was published in the *Human Development Report* and sums up the dilemma that we face in the development field. In 1960, the richest fifth of humanity had an income thirty times greater than the poorest fifth of humanity. In 1990, thirty years later, the richest fifth of humanity had an income sixty times greater than the poorest fifth of humanity. The gap is widening between the rich and the poor.

If you go to India, a country that I visit often, you see 100 million people in India who have a tremendous standard of living, but there are 800 million people in India who have virtually nothing. It's the same in Indonesia and in many of the developing countries. The gap between the rich and the poor is also widening in my own country of Canada.

When the fiftieth anniversary document says that the new agenda must greatly reduce and eventually eliminate poverty, I say, yes. But how will we "greatly reduce" poverty unless a great deal more of the resources now available are put into the alleviation of distress, the development of the human person at the local level through education and health? How are we going to get any form of equity established unless more of the resources are aimed at developing people who are at the bottom of the economic ladder?

RM: We need urgently a world budget to determine what is being spent on what. When I was director of the U.N. budget for a time, I made comparisons between the United Nations budget and national budgets: what is being spent on the military, what is being spent on education. The duplication and waste between nations are simply colossal. The astronomic military expenditures could be used for productive purposes. We have to rethink the entire world spending and economy. In fact, we have to rethink the whole administration of the planet.

DR: One of the ways in which we can do this rethinking is to examine the relationship between disarmament and development. Here the United Nations has made a tremendous contribution through the 1980s, starting with the report of Inga Thorssen on the relationship between disarmament and development, which led to the conference of the same name in 1987. As the final document of that conference clearly shows, there is a dynamic triangular relationship between disarmament, development, and security. The more you advance disarmament and development, the more security is enhanced and strengthened. Resources released from disarmament ought to be applied to development.

What happened was that the major nations paid lip service to this—leaving aside the question of the United States boycotting the conference on the grounds that there is no relationship. There is still a resistance in the North to recognizing that the resources applied to defense procurement and weapons buildups—even with the end of the Cold War—are constraining their ability to put the same resources into development in the name of security. Most nations haven't yet made the mental leap that security today requires the development of the human being, not just the preparation for war.

RM: We really need mental jumps to break through all the obstacles, all the wrong thinking, all the mistakes, which make the world look chaotic, where nobody understands anymore where we are going. We must make a mental leap into the third millennium, we must have the courage to say what is fundamentally wrong, what is antiquated, and what has become contrary to the fulfillment of human life and the preservation of the planet. This is fundamental. I'm glad that at least the fiftieth anniversary of the U.N. is a way of reviewing the past and looking into the future.

DR: To attack poverty, as the secretary-general himself noted in his document, "An Agenda for Development," we've got to deal with the provision of basic social services, employment generation, food security, drug and transnational crime control, and access to credit, technology, training, and markets.[1] That is a large agenda. The Social Summit, dealing with its three themes of poverty, unemployment, and lack of social integration, reflects advances being made in thinking in U.N. circles. Is the idea that has been proposed for a Security Council for Development to parallel the existing Security Council, which deals with peace and security questions, a good one? Should a Security Council for Development deal with all the development issues in an integrated manner to give them a higher priority?

RM: I believe that we have to uplift the priority of human fulfillment. The Economic and Social Council, of which I was the secretary for a number of years, is fine, but it is not enough. In the U.N., we get good reports from the thirty-two specialized agencies, but we do not have a place where a policy-making body can deal with the future with an interdependent, holistic view. This is missing. Perhaps we should reduce the Security Council to the level of the Economic and Social Council and lift the Economic and Social Council to be the number one organ of the United Nations. After all, security and defense ought to promote the security and happiness of people. Why don't we put fulfillment as the priority item on the new agenda and not armaments for the military?

---

1. Boutros Boutros-Ghali, *An Agenda for Development* (New York: United Nations Department of Public Information, 1995).

The mere idea of proposing a Security Council in the economic and social field is a good one. At the beginning of the economic development process, we did have the concept of basic needs. It has lost ground over the years. The priority ought not to be to provide people with automobiles but to fulfill their basic needs for food, water, employment, education, and health. We must return to this again as a first priority. Also, we now have the concept of sustainable development. We cannot go beyond the limits of the planet. We must not devastate it. President Figueres of Costa Rica was successful in getting the summit meeting of American heads of states in Miami to put sustainable development as a priority in the future.

DR: The words "sustainable development" make me nervous. I understand the concept, as Mrs. Bruntland originally intended it, but I do not think that sustainable development on the planet is possible unless there is an enormous change made in the lifestyles of the rich.

RM: You are absolutely right. But it marks a progress. When I look at my time at the U.N., if someone had told me in 1948 that one day people would speak about sustainable development, I would have been astonished. The exploitation of development through science and technology and conquering the world's resources were viewed as having no limits. We have at least damped that viewpoint.

DR: Progress since then has made us face the ultimate issue: our economy demands escalating consumer consumption in order to be successful, and escalating consumer consumption with a drainage of resources is bringing us crashing against the limitations of a biosphere that is already cracking under the strain of swelling populations and resource depletion and pollution. That problem is surely going to be evident in the next millennium. "Sustainable development" ought to mean addressing this problem now.

RM: The question of overconsumption, of wasteful consumption in millions of homes, has only emerged recently. Before that, people didn't even speak about it. It is shocking that there are only so few countries with a consumer protection agency or a ministry of consumption. It is all production, energy, transport, development, economic growth. How about the destruction of the planet, the depletion of its resources, of its nature, its miraculous biodiversity, the product of billions of years of evolution?

DR: I want to speak to you about the subject of the famous 0.7 percent of gross national product to be applied to official development assistance. This is the United Nations target by which the OECD countries measure their contribution to the development process. I have mixed feelings about the efficacy of 0.7 percent. Nonetheless, the appeal was renewed at the Earth Summit, not to mention other important international conferences lately. Today, only the following countries have reached 0.7 percent in ODA: the Netherlands, Sweden, Norway, and Denmark. The remaining OECD countries are way down the scale and, in fact, the average is now less than 0.3 percent. Is the maintenance of the target set by the U.N. of 0.7 percent a sound strategy? Does it divert us from the attention needed to change the rules for fairer international competition that are marginalizing the poorest nations?

When one looks at Africa, for instance, it is the recipient of a great deal of aid, doubtless not enough, but it is because Africa cannot trade and does not receive sufficient job-producing investment, that its export figures are extremely low. It suffers the weight of value-added inflation for its importations. It can never get out from behind the eight-ball. This applies to a number of Asian nations and certain Latin American states also. So I wrestle with whether or not we need to maintain 0.7 percent as evidence of our bona fides, or is it diverting us from politically attacking the causes of poverty, which are the unfair and discriminatory international trading and financial regulations?

RM: I remember when this came up in the postwar debate on economic development. At that time, we considered one percent as a target. The target was mostly a political image to get people accustomed to at least a minimum of aid going to the people of developing countries. I don't recall it being a rational or calculated policy. Rather than focusing on such a target, the public ought to consider how to provide and protect the essentials: water, air, land, food, dwellings, nature, animal friends. The biosphere of this miraculous planet is so fragile and so full of wonders that when you look at the behavior of governments, politicians, and of all kinds of professions doing the wrong things, you have the impression you live in a madhouse.

DR: There are fresh ideas for new sources of money to stimulate the development process in the secretary-general's "Agenda for Development." He points to a fee on speculative international financial transactions. Because of the multi-billions of dollars that are traded every twenty-four hours in the global trading market, the smallest taxation would hardly be noticed. He talks about a levy on fossil fuel use or its resulting pollution. That would certainly be a new source of funding. He talks about earmarking a small portion of the anticipated decline in world military expenditures. Also, utilizing some of the resources that could be released through the elimination of unnecessary subsidies. And, finally, a tax on international travel. Those are ideas that would foster, were they to be implemented, a greater sharing of resources between the developed and developing world in ways that would not hurt the developed world.

Just mentioning these areas where new money for development purposes could be obtained points up the dilemma we face: how to develop a shared vision of the instrumentalities to support the common desire for peace and security. This subject returns us to the spiritual dimension or the ethical basis of the human security problems. It isn't that we don't have enough money for development. It isn't that we don't have sufficient resources. It isn't that we don't have enough information on how to do this. What we lack is the will, the love, the humanity to move forward together.

RM: When the Cold War ended, it was said that private enterprise was going to solve everything. Then the World Social Summit had to be convened because the gap between the rich and the poor has increased everywhere. Now it is time for a global commission on a new economics. We have to make several mental jumps to see whether after two hundred years of classical economics we do not need something new. The environment has begun to teach us a lesson which we must heed.

DR: The Human Development Report has done much to raise the level of understanding about the true criteria for development. We are learning that, just as poverty is destructive, superabundance is destructive in its own ways. To achieve a balance between the rich and the poor is to bring us directly to the spirituality of the human being. You have cited several global commissions you would like to see. I would like to see a global commission on spirituality as a basis for our planetary development with peace, equality, justice, and development.

RM: Our spirituality has been lost sight of, partly because of the wars of the religions and their injustices, so that there was a revolution against religion and spirituality. The mistake which we made in development was to start with economics (*oikos, nomos*)—how to manage and exploit our home (the planet) before knowing fully our home. The ecology (*oikos, logos*) or proper knowledge of our planet with its interdependence should have been first. Beyond this, we will soon enter a new age of values, of ethics, of philosophy (the meaning of life on this planet), and of spirituality (our meaning in the universe and in time). We possess already a global brain and a global nervous system, but we still need a global heart and a global soul. At least, we do not live in a dull time!

CHAPTER 6

Global Education as a Basis of Hope

DR: We live at a transformation moment in world history. Several dimensions reveal that we are entering a wholly new period in history. First, there is a physical, technological transformation, by which we now see the interdependencies linking us wherever we are in the world: the environmentalists, the global traders, the sweep of democracy across borders.

The end of the Cold War is a dramatic illustration of the transformation moment. Thanks to the new enlightenment brought about particularly in the 1980s through the series of world commissions by Brandt, Palme, Bruntland, and Nyerere, there is an understanding of common security. The old militarism that produced enormous arms buildups was not a contribution to security but insecurity. There is now a whole new way of thinking about security.

The fiftieth anniversary of the United Nations, marking half a century of the world body, the only place where the entire world comes together to sort out its problems, occurring on the eve of the third millennium, reminds us of the power of this transformation moment and of the U.N. as a house of transformation. It has also deepened our understanding of the integral humanism that marks us as human beings. We know one another as we were never able to know one another before. Communications and transportation are mechanisms to facilitate this.

Finally, we understand now that the individual on the planet is related to every other individual, and we are related to the planet as a whole.

The combination of these illustrations of transformation makes this the most powerful moment in history. That is why this moment of the fiftieth anniversary of the United Nations ought not to be lost. For me, this underscores the spirituality, which is at the basis of the problems and the solutions for the continuance of development of the planet in security and safety. We must understand, at this transformation moment, where we have come from—from a creator. It's in commonality, global commonality, that we can now plan our destiny. This is an empowering and enriching moment.

RM: Let me put it in two ways, which are convergent. The first one is a current that comes from the scientists, and the other is the one which comes from the United Nations.

It is very interesting that, in the last few decades, most scientists have held a pessimistic view of the future. Many said that evolution doesn't make sense. There is the theory of chaos, that the universe is a kind of chaos and that humans are aberrations in evolution. A physicist astronomer, Fred Hoyle, held the view that humans developed the brain because we were not strong enough with our hands to fight other animals. So the brain was just another instrument to compensate our shortcomings in violence.

In latter years, there has been a change. I suggested that UNESCO hold a conference of long-term evolutionary scientists, like physicists, biologists, astro-physicists, anthropologists, paleonthologists, to determine the current proportion of pessimists and optimists. I think the number of optimists has increased because of the birth of a global consciousness. That consciousness, that global brain, is the new evolutionary phase that will help humanity to become probably the most advanced species that has ever existed.

This is why the United Nations holds one world conference after the other to enlighten people, to probe our new ways. Eminent global persons outside the United Nations, who are not hampered by political obstacles, give us a tremendous view of what the world can be in the next century. I would say this is not only a turning point in history, it is a turning point in evolution.

DR: I'm struck by your notion that, despite the massiveness of problems, the world can "make it." The birth of a global consciousness is now—even though much too slowly—spreading through important circles. Having expressed the optimism I feel about this elevation of human understanding of ourselves, I have immediately to conjoin that with my deep concern about the state of the pillars for global security today. Measured in terms of disarmament, or the development process of the poorest peoples of the world, or environment, these three pillars are shaky. They need to be shored up. I doubt that the political process, left to itself, will shore up these three pillars to make them strong enough to take us well into the twenty-first century.

We must tell our politicians not to be afraid of spirituality as a base for public policy formation. We must recognize that we need new models of coexistence among the various cultures and races and religions that now operate within a single interconnected civilization. If we could muster sufficient strength to push the political process in that direction to ensure that we get an enduring security and lead to the abolition of war as a means of conflict resolution—then my personal optimism will increase.

RM: We do need a spiritual renaissance on this planet. The year 2000 gives us an opportunity to do it. The pope is preparing a kind of spiritual renaissance as revealed in his recent book, *Crossing the Threshold of Hope*, and in his apostolic letter on the third millennium.[1] These explorations may yet culminate in what the great prophets and religious leaders have always foreseen.

When I was child, life for me was a miracle—the stars, the trees, the birds were all incredibly beautiful. I went to church in the morning to hear an old organ player, and I was in communion with the universe and with eternity in that church. Then came education. Education killed all this. Spirituality was totally excluded in France. It was anticlerical, and what I had to learn was the geography and history of France, its victories, its heroes, its literature, etc. Then the Germans came, and it was the opposite story. Then I went to the United States where I had to learn economics. The purpose of life was to make money and to create prosperity.

When I joined the United Nations I couldn't believe that I found a Dag Hammarskjold who, from an economist, had been transformed into a mystic. He was writing a marvellous book, *Markings*, a dialogue with God.[2] Then I had even a greater privilege in working with U Thant, the Burmese Buddhist, who always

---

1. Pope John Paul II, *Crossing the Threshold of Hope* (New York: Knopf, 1994).
2. Dag Hammarskjold, *Markings* (New York: Knopf, 1964).

said to me, "Robert, why do you separate spirituality from life? Life is spirituality from morning to evening. You Westerners make a mistake by putting it in the church on Sunday. Every human being is unique whom you must respect. He is a creation of the universe, something absolutely unique."

Having learned this, I myself became a spiritual being because of all the knowledge I received from the United Nations—from the infinitely large to the infinitely small, the total knowledge of our planet, the total knowledge of humanity, the total knowledge of our journey from the infinite past to the future. It took me a number of years to sort this out to get this Copernican enlightenment, which I have described in my book *New Genesis: Shaping a Global Spirituality*.[3] One day I said, my God, this is exactly what Jesus said, what the Buddha said, what all the great prophets and saints said in simple, moving terms without even knowing that the world was round, without having a theory of the galaxies. The period we are arriving at now through possession of our knowledge of the universe from the infinitely large to the infinitely small, encourages an incredible respect for the miracle which this universe and humanity represent with the consciousness of our environment, I'm absolutely sure that we will see a unique revival of spirituality. In my *Testament to the U.N.* I have a whole chapter on the U.N. and spirituality.[4]

The problem is that most religions believe that they have the ultimate truth. They must share their truths and express a global truth. What do all religions have in common? This is the great new spirituality. You can have different gods, different rituals, different pilgrimages, as we have different beliefs, languages, and

---

3. Robert Muller, *Genesis: Shaping a Global Spirituality* (Anacortes, Wash.: World Happiness and Cooperation, 1982).

4. Robert Muller, *My Testament of the U.N.* (Anacortes, Wash.: World Happiness and Cooperation, 1992).

cultures. Unity in diversity must be brought to the fore among the religions, too.

DR: "A unique revival of spirituality." Again I find you using words that are extremely powerful because they can move the forces of humanity. We have begun to see such movement. The taking down of the Berlin Wall was, as Vaclav Havel said, not a victory of one side over the other in the prolonged Cold War but the result of a quest by humanity for authentication of values, in this case of freedom and democracy. In this search for spirituality or even a revival of spirituality, we can see ways in which a value system can be introduced into our public policy formation. What are the bonds, the values that bond us irrespective of where we are? Is it too much to ask the politicians to express those elements in terms of the fact that we are rooted in the earth as a common people and also rooted in the cosmos? Is it too much to ask them to respect the miracle of the universe and the miracle of our own existence? Is it too much to ask them to understand that our future as a human species must be rooted in self transcendence in which we are reaching to the earth and the cosmos at the same time?

Now I answer my own questions. And I say it's too much. Certainly in this period of history. There isn't enough education. There isn't enough public information. There's too much manipulation. The corporate barons still control, through their manipulative techniques, what we think as a public.

But I don't give up because I think there is a value that does transcend our divisions. I think that irrespective of what perspective we bring to the elements of peace, equality, justice, and development, there is a common moral principle that can be applied to the basis of all of them—and that is the principle of reciprocity. Reciprocity is nothing new. Confucius taught reciprocity. Jesus taught reciprocity through the Golden Rule. Simply, it's this:

"Do not do unto others that which you do not want done to yourself." I ask myself why this moral principle that has endured through the ages cannot now be applied to the subjects of nuclear weapons, poverty, destruction of the environment. Why could not reciprocity become a new basis for national policies, given our enlightened understanding of our relationship to one another on the earth that sweeps by national sovereignties?

RM: It brings me back to spirituality because, in thinking about the principle of reciprocity, I am immediately reminded of U Thant. That was his basic rule of life. The Hindus call it the karma. If you do good, you will produce more good. If you hate, if you do evil, it will create hatred and evil. His daily life was to be good and to do good. It reminds me that in this revival of spirituality in the world, there are elements which make me hopeful.

First, we have models, e.g., Hammarskjold, who, from an economist, became a mystic in the U.N. U Thant, a totally spiritual secretary-general on the basis of his humble approach to life via karma, via the heart. Perez de Cuellar was the third spiritual secretary-general, via art and beauty. He was a spiritual person because he saw the miracle of life and all the beauty surrounding us created by music and art. I have previously mentioned Robert Schuman, who was a living saint in politics. We need to study, revere, and emulate people like these. We must offer them as models to young people.

Second, there is the fact that communism has disappeared and is no longer here to oppose a spiritual renaissance and discussion at the United Nations. The preparatory committee for the World Social Summit in Copenhagen dealt with the problem of spirituality. Also, there was the World Parliament of Religions with its powerful statement on global ethics. And recently, Harold Stassen, the last living U.S. signer of the charter, recommended in his redraft of the charter for the fiftieth anniversary that the United Nations hold a yearly conference of all religious leaders. Five years ago, this would have been unthinkable. The year 2000 can be a tremendous turning point in revival of spirituality in the world.

True, there are great obstacles—such as corporate greed and media diversion. But the principle of reciprocity, the principle of karma in relations between all entities—families, corporations, cities, nations—is quite essential.

DR: I see reciprocity as a place where spiritual values and the pragmatics that drive our time intersect. It seems to me that even policy makers, who would disclaim or put aside discussions of spirituality, are capable of understanding the benefits of reciprocity. This subject returns us once more to the central dilemma that is in my mind. Even though I have a tremendous desire to find and express hope, there is this cloud in my mind that the forces of the powerful that have driven world history are not about to be denied just because we are transformed into a new era. Unless, of course, they are overcome by a sweep of humanity.

Applying reciprocity to nuclear weapons, it seems to me that it is logical to say I will not aim a nuclear weapon at you because I don't want you to aim one at me. When I look at such instruments as the Non-Proliferation Treaty as a means for eliminating nuclear weapons and introduce into that the concept of reciprocity, logic tells me that all sides should move to the abolition of nuclear weapons. But I do not believe this is happening—certainly not happening yet or within agreed time frames because we have not yet been able to overcome the determination of the strong to control.

As we conclude our conversation, we cannot wrap all these subjects up in a nice box with a red ribbon around it, like a nice Christmas present. Life is messy and cannot be put together into a neat package. The people whom we are addressing in this dialogue need to be encouraged, not feel diminished or defeated because they can't get it all neatly tied up.

I used the illustration of nuclear weapons to show how hard it would be to get reciprocity even as a basic common value introduced into the international system. But if we can make advances in our understanding of why reciprocity makes sense as a common value, that will open the way to reconciliation, which I do see as a higher spiritual value—one that is lost in the savagery of the ethnic conflicts that scar our world today. Reconciliation flowing out of the enlarged understanding of who and what we are in this elevated world is something for us to aim at.

RM: I received recently an outline of a thesis from a young American student who wrote that she had been asked to write on conflict resolution. She said she was sick and tired of hearing about conflict resolution, that everywhere there are hundreds of such theses, and she had come to the conclusion that the best way to avoid conflict and to resolve conflict is to have common aims. I congratulated her for writing a thesis on common endeavours for the good of humanity as the best way to prevent conflicts.

DR: Just as a married couple has to have reconciliation in the daily flow of their lives, so a family, even the global family, has to have the principle and value of reconciliation in order for them to get on with healing the hurts that we give one another. This concept of advancing the prospect of human reconciliation ought not to be too much at the United Nations. I've often felt, standing at the front of the General Assembly, seeing the faces of the world that are represented, that that itself is a sort of a reconciling.

I would illustrate this with an anecdote. I was struck one evening at a dinner of U.N. ambassadors when the Soviet ambassador took a picture out of his wallet of a new grandchild.

Everybody congratulated him on the new grandchild. The American ambassador, not to be outdone, took out a picture of his three grandchildren. Here were the Soviet ambassador and the American ambassador, at the height of the Cold War, saying to each other and the dinner table, that we have to work for peace for these children. We toasted all the grandchildren of the world. Of course, the next day they were back in committee, reflecting their national policies, tearing each other apart. But, at the human level, those two men were ready for reconciliation. That's for me a poignant story about how we can reach out with a healing hand and take those practical steps to effect reconciliation.

As you move to the larger scene, I think reconciliation requires a vastly improved education system. We need global education to help young people particularly. Although I don't refer exclusively to the young when I speak of education and I certainly do not speak exclusively of academia, education must concentrate on the young. This would be supplemented in the enlarged networks of communications and NGO systems through which we develop public opinion and global consciousness. That's what needs to be enlarged today in order to infuse the public and the future public with the elements of who we are in an integrated world in which we now see our human relationships.

RM: Your anecdote of the grandchildren prompts me to add that children are the biggest binding element of human reconciliation. They are our common interest in the future.

My ideal of education would be to give children good information, rationally and beautifully presented, about the greatness of the planet from the infinitely large to the infinitely small, and the entire human family, its races, religions, ethnic groups, languages, and so on. After the magnificent diversity of nature and the diversity of humans, the next step is to show them our place in time. Help them come to the conclusion that the purpose of their life is to contribute to the incredible, wonderful story of the planet, so that when they close their eyes they can say: my life has been worthwhile. Unfortunately, this is not taught to children.

Education today markets profits and greed instead of marketing life. We advertise products instead of teaching the art of living. But this is beginning to to be challenged too. I have been struck that during the last year, when meeting a number of wealthy businessmen, I asked them: "Are you satisfied with your life?", their answer was: "I'm not satisfied with my life. I have the impression that I have lost my life. I am still looking for my way." When you hear a man who is in his fifties, who has made a fortune in petroleum or things like this, tell you, "I am looking for my way," it means that he begins to consider his life as unsuccessful.

DR: Education is the base of all that we are advancing as a reason for extending hope for the human condition. One of the reasons that I left public life after some eighteen years was to devote myself to expanding global education. For a long time, at least in our country, we've had what's called development education. That is, we tried to educate people about why the North should help the South. As we have come to understand in greater maturity the interdependencies of how we are all affected one way or another irrespective of where we live, I have begun to favour the term "global education" because it reflects more the holistic nature of the world. And here I find a paramount reason for hope. We have had from the great religions, traditions of the world, the cultures coming down through the centuries—what I might call the vertical track—the admonition that we should love one another. This is not confined to any one religion; it has been a general admonition. To that is now conjoined a horizontal track which I call the pragmatic track, brought about by the increase in technological developments of the world that tell us we have to get along. We have to love. We have to know. We have to understand. We have to be sensitive. I have to understand that the woman in Bangladesh is my sister. That the farmer in Kerala is my brother. Those are the new dimensions brought about by pragmatics. So the conjoining of the vertical and the horizontal track empower this very moment for holistic education based on, as the philosopher Jacques Maritain said, integral humanism. When the integral humanism is seen in the light of the integrated security agenda of disarmament, development, and environment protection, we can enlarge the basis for a stronger spirituality flowing from holistic global education.

RM: In 1970, on the twenty-fifth anniversary, I was working with U Thant, the Buddhist secretary-general, who was a schoolmaster in his country. And in our private conversations, he always came back to this statement: "Robert, we will not have world peace if we do not have a new education on this planet." He really believed in this and that is why he advocated the creation of a United Nations University and of a University for Peace. In his Buddhist spirituality and simplicity, he reminded me of the education which I received when I was a child. Here I had the contact with the vertical, which you just mentioned. I loved as a little boy to go to the mass at dawn because in the church I got the feeling of being in communion with the universe, with heaven. This is what the priest and the organ-player through his music conveyed to me.

Today, after many years, I've come to the conclusion that the only correct education I received in my life was from the United Nations itself. There I was given a total view of the universe, of the whole planet, the whole humanity, of their diverse compo-nents, of the changes in time, and of our future evolution.

DR: I want to affirm strongly what you have just said about the United Nations being your educator. The United Nations has also been my teacher. Studying the areas of disarmament, devel-opment, and the environment as the three components for a global security agenda has enriched my understanding and appreciation of the world community. I think that professional educators especially ought to be encouraged to realize that global education is not so much a subject as a perspective. Cer-tainly, there are some subjects that lend themselves particularly to global education, but the processes of opening up the human mind to an awareness of our role in the planet is at the basis of global education. Some fears have been expressed that this is a left-wing agenda and that it will result in diminished patriotism. Actually, global education, properly done, can help to extend appreciation of one's country, the blessings, and whatever is hap-pening in one's own country—but not at the expense of every other country. There need not be a tension between educating for civic responsibilities in a domestic setting and educating for civic responsibilities in a global setting. The nature of our com-munity of life today is, in fact, the world.

I would even argue further that not to prepare young people for this kind of experience, which is going to become overwhelm-ing for them in the twenty-first century, is to deny them the kind of education they need to survive. Those who say, we are only going to educate young people to get them ready for a job are themselves denying their charges of that which they need. Global education, properly implemented, can lead to the understanding and appreciation of a new global ethic. A knowledge of history and understanding of the evolving unity of the planet, along with a vision of social justice and true human security, are the essential qualities that a human being needs in order to be educated to live peacefully in the next millennium.

RM: I was witness to much killing and horrors during World War II as a young man. I could not believe that humans could do this to each other—always in the name of a nation, in the name of a flag. I was given a rifle to shoot in one direction and when the others took over I was given the rifle to shoot exactly in the opposite direction. I have come to the conclusion that life is superior to any nation, to any group, to any patriotism. If I lose my life, they will throw my passport in the waste basket. But if I throw my passport in the waste basket, I'm still alive. Life is superior to any political consideration. I have claimed, in one of my books, a new human right, the fundamental human right not to kill and not to be killed, not even in the name of a nation. We must have the courage to say this. I expect my nation, if it has a quarrel with another one, to resolve it by peaceful means—not by asking me to kill these other people. Why do they do this to me? They have no right. Nations exist to protect my life, not to use it up.

DR: This is to bring us, as we near the end of our dialogue, to the subject of leadership. I must be frank. I do not have confidence that the kind of world we are aspiring to will be brought about by a leader arriving on the scene and getting up some morning, and saying, "Today, we are going to have a better world." I don't want to impute maliciousness to all political leaders, and I certainly do not want to imply disrespect for the high office that leaders, political and religious, occupy. But I have come to the conclusion, based on my own experience in parliamentary and diplomatic life, that the constraints of leadership are very real—whether they come from their own lack of vision or the chains of bureaucracies that entangle them, or from the sources of money that brought them to power in the first place. Whatever it is, I think that we have reached a new moment of leadership in the world that is also part of this transformation that I spoke about.

This is a moment when our leadership is horizontal. Our leadership is coming from swelling numbers of informed, committed, dedicated, non-governmental organizations that have now begun to make such an imprint on the world. We have seen this accelerate with the growth of the U.N. conferences on all the global subjects. I would not go so far as to say that the power of the people has become the determining factor in public policy formation. But it is certainly an increasing influence.

As global education widens its horizons, as nongovernmental organizations grow in strength and diversity (and, I say parenthetically, learn to work together better than they have in the past), this power or synergy of human energy arising in a world of great communication and transportation enables a new influence to be felt. This is a new kind of leadership that the elected political leadership and even the leadership in the churches will have to respond to. We are here now at the University for Peace, but there are countless numbers at work around the world. The cumulative effect of all this is to foster an ethic for change. Coming from the people, it will be greater in its effect than waiting for a new leader on the mountain.

RM: One has to look for leadership in every direction. It is wonderful if we have leaders who have the vision to try to change the world. Some of them even have special ways to do it. Franklin Roosevelt, in order to beat the bureaucracy, had the marvelous technique of surrounding himself with what he called "idea men." They put forward new ideas, like the United Nations, the Marshall Plan, the UNDP. There are not many great leaders because most of them are satisfied to be the president of a country, forgetting what kind of a president. There are so many presidents in the world today that it is very difficult to become famous and to leave an impact on world history.

Also, let's not underestimate institutions because very often an institution is able to have an impact which people do not have. The European Union has forced the Germans and French to get together and now they begin to like it. They like to cross the border to have a glass of wine on the German side, and the others come to the French side to have an Alsatian meal. Here was an institution ahead of the people. Norway voted against joining the European Community. The government wanted it, the institution of Europe was ready to accommodate it, but the people were not yet ready. As a general philosophy, one must say that institutions are not alive. Institutions are shells, they are mechanisms without a life of their own. It is only people who have life.

The United Nations charter starts with the words, "We the peoples" and the next sentence refers to governments. Although "We the peoples" created the U.N., it is governments which have taken it over. People practically disappeared from the United Nations except through their representatives. In time, NGO representatives were permitted to submit papers to the Economic and Social Council. This led to an explosion of non-governmental organizations accredited to the U.N. Now, NGOs are all around the U.N. buttonholing the delegates, coming up with their own ideas and resolutions.

Margaret Mead proposed that whenever the U.N. has a world conference, NGOs should have a parallel one. At the Earth Summit in Rio de Janeiro, the heads of states and delegates were greatly outnumbered by NGOs. The same phenomenon will occur at the Beijing women's conference. The push forward of nongovernmental organizations is extraordinary. The secretary-general strongly supported the new NGO enlargement. I have come to the conclusion that we should now institutionalize this with a People's Assembly. At least, let the people speak. Also, let us do what they did in Europe, create a consultative United Nations parliamentary assembly. The European experience later led to direct parliamentary election of European representatives.

DR: This is the note of hope and practicality that I think we now strike at the end of our conversation. The words, "We the peoples of the United Nations," which open the charter, have been trampled on by governments, greed and wars through fifty years. Nonetheless, there is alive today a growing desire to make of the United Nations more than a place where governments come with all their national outlooks and priorities.

It was this very experience that I underwent as a parliamentarian, being shut out of the decision-making processes of the U.N., that led me to become a founder of Parliamentarians for Global Action in 1980. The organization now numbers 1,110 parliamentarians in 81 countries, dedicated to the processes of conferences and lobbying and access to government policymaking machinery to strengthen global security by shoring up the pillars of disarmament, development, and the environment. In some 15 years, that organization has become an important instrument with significant accomplishments.

All of this has been preparatory to what must come, and that is a Parliamentary Assembly of the United Nations by direct election. Just as you had direct election to the European Parliament—something which they said in Europe twenty or thirty years ago would never happen—we must aim for a Parliamentary Assembly at the United Nations by direct election. Perhaps it will come by appointment of existing parliamentarians at the beginning, but later it will evolve into direct election. As a sign of hope, I point to the Canadian Parliament, where the Committee on Foreign Affairs made this as a principal recommendation a year ago, asking the Canadian government to lead the way by establishing conferences that would be aimed at the development of the parliamentary assembly for the United Nations. This is part of the horizontalization of leadership.

Being at the University For Peace these last few days has had a profound effect on me because being here, not exactly in solitude but in quiet, and with a certain special bonding with nature in its glories around us, has freed my mind of much of the daily clatter that prevents one from taking a long view of how we can proceed with the development of God's planet. For me, these days have been a blessing, and I only wish that I could extend that blessing into the millions and billions.

RM: Your visit and few days here have been a blessing to me and to this university. As we look out the window, we can see the first monument on this planet to unknown peacemakers. It was a dream of U Thant who once complained to me that in each capital he visited he was asked to light a flame at a monument to an unknown soldier but never at a monument to an unknown peacemaker. The monument points at the rising sun. This is a place from which miracles emerge, one after the other, fulfilling an ancient prophecy in a beautiful indigenous legend we found here: In the little village near the university called formerly Quisur, one day the children disappeared underground. The parents could not understand it: there were no caves in the area. The children were laughing and singing. They began to move under the earth towards this hill. The parents followed them. At one point, they were stopped by a strong magnetic force. The children then reappeared from under the Earth, as well as a being of resplendent light, Rasur, the indigenous God of the children. He talked to the children, never turning to the parents, and told them that God was in every tree, every flower, every butterfly, every animal, and that the children should take good care of them, to love them. At the end of his speech, before disappearing, he prophesied that from these hills a civilization of peace would extend to the entire world.

Well, it is here that Jose Figueres camped with his insurgent troops (we found the site) and conceived the dream of demilitarizing Costa Rica to preserve its magnificent natural beauty. It is here that the first University for Peace on this planet is now located. It is here that there is the First International Radio for Peace. And it is here that the Earth Council created by the U.N. Rio de Janeiro Conference on the environment will soon move. Here also, recently, a Dutch lady philanthropist, Elinore Detiger, bought land next to the university to establish a center and retreat house for teachers, to learn about the world core curriculum and the Robert Muller schools which were born from my many years of experience and observation at the United Nations.

We named the grounds of the university the Gardens of Quisur. One day young geomancists (earth force measurers) came from New Zealand to measure the telluric and cosmic forces emanating from these grounds.

They found them to be very strong, strongest at the place where we erected the monument to Gandhi. We did not give much credence to their science and findings until we were told by the director of the Costa Rican LACS airlines that pilots avoided overflying the area of the university because of magnetic disturbances affecting their instruments!

The waves, the dreams, the prophecy, the spirits, and energy which emanate from this sacred place are immense signs of hope. Our beautiful monument to peace is built in the form of a spiral because the spiral extends to the entire universe. We hope that it will extend Costa Rica's demilitarization, peace, and beautiful environment to the entire world. May you be one of the messengers of Rasur and a gardener of Quisur. May the energy which bathed you here never leave you and produce miracles wherever you will be.

CHAPTER 7

A Blueprint for Action

The fiftieth anniversary of the United Nations is, of course, a time for reflection on what has been accomplished in the first half century. The challenges we set out in this blueprint for action, which may seem audacious to some, should be seen in the context of what has already been accomplished, the problems notwithstanding. We are including a list of U.N. achievements in the Appendix to widen understanding of the U.N.'s many successes and to provide inspiration for action to achieve a new round of goals for the second half-century.

We are convinced there is a momentum building up around the world for the implementation of the common security agenda as the basis for a new world order.

The long history of the world, characterized by the quest for domination, has reached a higher plateau where, for the first time, the intermingling of intellectualism, technology, and danger provide both motivation and means for common survival. It is this very ability to assess that provides the human family with its new power.

This spirit of hope is brilliantly caught in the report of the
Commission on Global Governance, chaired by Prime Minister
Ingvar Carlsson of Sweden and Shridath Ramphal, former secretary-general of the Commonwealth.1 Their report emphasizes
that global governance, once viewed primarily as concerned
with intergovernmental relationships, now involves not only
governments but also nongovernmental organizations, citizens'
movements, transnational corporations, academia, and the mass
media. The emergence of a global civil society, with many movements reinforcing a sense of human solidarity, reflects the
dynamic character of NGOs.

> The emergence of a global civil society, with many move-
> ments reinforcing the sense of human solidarity, is one of
> the most positive features of our time. It reflects a large
> increase in the capacity and will of people to take control of
> and improve their own lives.

The Commission on Global Governance, like a growing
number of contemporary analysts, believes that the problems of
a sustainable future on the planet are so deep that only a new,
elevated humanism can engender lasting solutions.

> We believe that a global civic ethic to guide action within
> the global neighbourhood and leadership infused with that
> ethic are vital to the quality of global governance. We call
> for a common commitment to core values that all humanity
> could uphold: respect for life, liberty, justice and
> equity,mutual respect, caring, and integrity. We further
> believe humanity as a whole will be best served by recogni-
> tion of a set of common rights and responsibilities.

When President Vaclav Havel of the Czech Republic warns us
that "self-transcendence," i.e., reaching out to the human community, is "the only real alternative to extinction," he is uttering a

---

1. *Our Global Neighborhood: The Report of the Commission on Global Governance* (Oxford: Oxford University Press, 1995).

profound truth. This truth must be explored in the search for universal laws based on commonly held ethical values. Those values underlie the global search for peace, equality, justice, and development.

The reform of the U.N., then, is not just a political struggle; it is part of the advance of the human community into the new age. It requires vision and values impressed on the political process by those who would lift up humanity to share in the blessings of a provident world.

Moreover, Secretary-General Boutros Boutros-Ghali has appealed to nongovernmental organizations, academic institutions, parliamentarians, business and professional communities, the media, and the public at large to further the work of the United Nations.

> You are an essential part of the legitimacy without which no international activity can be meaningful. Often, it is you who, on a day-to-day basis, constitute the link between democracy and peace.

To make the point even sharper, he added:

> I wish to state It to you as clearly as possible—I need the mobilizing power of nongovernmental organizations.

The recommendations we suggest here, grouped to correspond to the elements of this book—peace, equality, justice, development, and global education—are a synthesis of our own ideas[2] along with those set out by Global Education Associates[3] and the World Federalist Association.[4]

---

2. Robert Muller, *Framework for Preparation for the Year 2000: The 21st Century and the Third Millenium* (Hamden, Conn.: Albert Einstein Institute/Quinnipac College Press, 1994).

3. *The United Nations in an Interdependent World: Past, Present, Future*, eds., Patricia M. Mische and Rosamond C. Rodman, Global Education Associates, New York, N.Y.

4. World Federalist Association, "Campaign for Global Change: Earth Governance 2010." Circulated as a paper.

PEACE

A GLOBAL SYSTEM TO ABOLISH WAR—*To establish and maintain an equitable system for eliminating war and strengthening peaceful means of conflict resolution, it is necessary to:*

1. Create a U.N. Arms Reduction Agency with the goal of lowering national armaments to the level required for domestic order.

2. Urge nations to adapt the proposals contained in Agenda for Peace for concrete measures to advance preventive diplomacy, peacemaking, peacekeeping, and peacebuilding. Special attention should be given to the Secretary-General's call for permanent peacekeeping forces under U.N. command and financed on a regular basis.

3. Democratize the Security Council by expanding the permanent seats in the Security Council so that they are more representative of the world's population than at present. Pay special attention to the need for stronger representation from Africa, Asia, and Latin America. Consider changing seats to regional representation with the possibility of term limits. Limit use of the veto.

4. Urge member governments to ratify existing treaties on disarmament, particularly the Convention on Chemical Weapons.

5. Create an Independent World Commission of Eminent Persons for the Abolition of Nuclear Weapons.

6. Urge the strengthening of the Non-Proliferation Treaty by the adoption of a specific time frame for the elimination of nuclear weapons.

7.   Make the U.N. Central Registry of Arms Transfers mandatory and expand it to include nuclear, chemical, and biological weapons, and dual-use technology. Use this as the basis for developing a binding treaty to impose limits on arms production and transfer.

EQUALITY

A DEMOCRATIC UNITED NATIONS—*To give a voice to the world's citizens and to institute more equitable, democratic and enforceable law-making and decision-making processes at the U.N., it is necessary to:*

1.   Create a more equitable voting system in the U.N. General Assembly.

2.   Create a parliamentary assembly of elected representatives at the U.N.

3.   Develop means for effective and credible participation of citizen organizations in the U.N. decision-making and operations.

4.   Overhaul political institutions and policies to root out discrimination against women. Increase the number of women in upper level management and occupational leadership.

5.   Give great priority to the role of women in economic and social development.

6.   Make a full range of educational opportunities accessible to women to maximize their quality of life and participation.

7.   Make reproductive health and family planning information available to all people.

8. Enhance access by youth nongovernmental organizations to information about youth participation and program within the U.N. system.

9. Create a U.N. Youth Corps of Volunteers for young people around the world wishing to assist a wide variety of U.N. programs.

10 Sponsor conferences on and for youth.

11. Encourage national governments to include youth in delegations for U.N.-sponsored world conferences, following the model established by the Nordic countries.

12. Create youth consultative groups and processes through which youth give input at regional and local levels.

13 Integrate human rights into all U.N. activities, and ensure the priority of human rights in the impact assessment of new projects.

14. Encourage all nations to develop an action plan stating how they will ensure the preservation of internationally recognized human rights.

15. Develop partnerships with NGOs. In the same way that they have contributed to standard setting and monitoring, NGOs should become partners in building human rights institutions, and in preventing human rights violations. International NGOs must also help in building and strengthening local NGOs because this is the level at which human rights promotion and protection must take place.

JUSTICE

A GLOBAL JUSTICE SYSTEM—*To extend the rule of law worldwide, protect the rights of individuals, peoples, corporate bodies, and nation-states, and to hold all accountable to international law, it is necessary to:*

1. Create a Global Bill of Rights based upon the U.N. Universal Declaration of Human Rights.

2. Create an International Criminal Court to try individuals and corporate bodies accused of violations of international law, such as terrorism, drug trafficking, genocide, war crimes, and gross abuses of human rights.

3. Provide the International Court of Justice with compulsory jurisdiction over disputes between nation-states.

4. Create a global development fund from resources diverted from arms production to raise the standard of living of the developing nations most in need.

5. Sign the "Earth Covenant," a citizens' treaty for common ecological security, already signed by more than one million people in eighty countries. The "Earth Covenant" is available from Global Education Associates, 475 Riverside Drive, Suite 1848, New York, New York 10015.

6. Improve the financial integrity of the U.N.:

   a) Consolidate emergency humanitarian assistance through one department.

   b) Establish a permanent, independent U.N. inspector general office in order to minimize waste and corruption and to establish accountability to the public.

    c)   Create procedures to enable staff to report financial misconduct without reprisal.

    d)   Provide special training to staff members with financial responsibilities.

7.   Develop stable, long-term funding for the U.N. system and its programs:

    a)   Charge interest on unpaid U.N. dues and assessments.

    b)   Suspend privileges of countries that are delinquent on these payments.

    c)   Tax international armaments sales, international currency trading, and transnational pollution of oceans and atmosphere.

8.   Establish a world consumers agency.

9.   Establish a world restoration agency.

10.   Transform the military into peace and environmental protectors, and shift world military expenditures.

DEVELOPMENT

A GLOBAL HUMAN DEVELOPMENT SYSTEM—*To promote human development in a manner which respects differences, ensures gender equity, promotes universal education and makes the health of the global family a top priority, it is necessary to:*

1.   Create a U.N. Commission on Social Development to develop and promote a new paradigm of human development, considering community quality of life issues such as education and health care.

2.   Reprioritize the lending practices of the international financial institutions toward sustainable, community-

based projects, and modify structural adjustments policies.

3. Transform the U.N. Fund for Population Activities into a U.N. specialized agency on population.

4. Create a World Marshall Plan for the improvement of the well being of the poor countries.

5. Design a world plan in which the European Community takes care of the development of Africa; North America (U.S., Canada) takes care of Latin America; and Japan, Australia, New Zealand, takes care of the poor areas of Asia.

6. Make the IMF and World Bank accountable for their projects by integrating them more fully within the U.N. system.

7. Develop a new Systems of Nations Accounts and broader quality-of-life indicators to provide a framework and criteria for development projects funded by U.N. agencies.

8. Integrate principles of the annual *Human Development Report* of the U.N. Development Program with those of the *World Development Report* of the World Bank.

9. Involve leaders in the social, physical, and humanistic sciences to join with economists in fashioning international trade agreements.

10. Press governments to implement *Agenda 21: The U.N. Program of Action on Sustainable Development*, the blueprint for action on environment and development going into the twenty-first century.

11. Pursue systematic action in cases of universal and pervasive harm caused by human technologies which upset natural systems.

12. Steer population and environmental policy development by the use of sound science.

13. Fund and undertake research on the relationship between environment, poverty, the status of women, child and infant mortality, and population.

14. Integrate national policies in the areas of the environment and population.

15. Initiate joint ventures and interagency programs on population issues.

16. Design a proper world migration policy.

17. Use labor in poor countries in manufacturing, health, and geriatric services.

18. Initiate a U.N. study of errors in transferring development models from the West to poor countries.

19. Hold an ILO-sponsored world conference on small and medium enterprises.

20. Proclaim an International Year of Villages and Rural Areas.

GLOBAL EDUCATION

NEW GLOBAL EDUCATION PRIORITIES—*To promote the advancement of a new global ethic based on our knowledge of history, on understanding the evolving unity of the planet, and on a vision of social justice and true human security, it is necessary to:*

1. Approach global education as a perspective, not a subject. Global education should underlie, shape, and harmonize the teaching and learning processes in schools. Through those processes, students develop

the values, knowledge, skills, and attitudes to participate in a world characterized by the many interdependencies. The global education approach enables students to examine critically the major issues affecting humankind and to participate actively in the society around them. Perhaps, most importantly, it seeks to foster in students certain attitudes:

- Curiosity, intellectual and cultural.
- Appreciation of diversity, receptivity to new perspectives, sense of commonality of humankind's needs, rights, aspirations, talents.
- Concern for justice, commitments to equality, defence of rights, their own and others'.
- Tolerance of uncertainty, conflict and change, ambiguity and "no easy answers" situations.
- Capacity for creativity, risk taking, thinking in images and symbols, and making or appreciating paradigm shifts.
- World awareness, holistic thinking, respect for life-forms and their place in the web of life.

2. Expand existing mechanisms which can empower educational institutions and networks to more easily make educational/instructional use of U.N. documents pertaining to global issues, e.g., human rights, environment, peace, world trade, intercultural education, etc. These educational tools should help to popularize and process U.N. conferences beyond the current NGO construct.

3. Incorporate an educational component into key U.N. documents with practical guidelines for curricular or extra-curricular use.

4. Develop adult education programs for the community and grassroots level. For example, secure, staff, and maintain U.N. mobile educational units, similar to Smithsonian travelling exhibitions. These could provide on-the-spot educational opportunities for people to learn about the U.N. system and to explore ways they can promote greater understanding of global interdependence and collaborate locally and regionally with U.N. agencies, programs, and conferences.

5. Work with international and national NGOs to encourage all countries to become active members of U.N. agencies, such as UNESCO, so that the country's educational organizations receive the U.N.'s educational materials.

6. Sponsor apprenticeship programs at U.N. conferences with students acting as interns.

7. Utilize the research and publications of the University for Peace and the U.N. University.

8. Establish and maintain, through UNESCO, a data base of global classroom ideas, practices, and pedagogies accessible to educational institutions and practitioners.

9. Recognize the contributions that religious networks can make to the development of a global ethic that respects religious differences, yet helps to provide a framework for responding to the global reality of our increasing interdependency.

10. Collaborate with religious institutions and networks to develop values and leadership for global systemic change.

11. Seek ongoing partnerships with religious institutions at local, national and regional levels to help advance research, community development projects and public education programs such as Education for All.

12. Utilize representatives, volunteers, and resource people from religious and multireligious networks in:

a) Peacemaking and peace-building efforts
(for example, in a multireligious negotiating force, a nonviolent training program,
and a Standing Peace Corps, humanitarian
emergency actions)

b) Local development programs (for example,
Education For All, and environmental sus-
tainability projects)

c) Humanitarian assistance

13. Establish a Religion Council for the U.N. that reports
directly to the Secretary-General, and has formal
liaisons with the specialized agencies and affiliated
organizations. The council's mandate would be:

a) To promote multireligious dialogue on issues
affecting the world's peoples and the planet.

b) To advise the U.N. on ethical and spiritual
values that can build global community.

c) To foster collaborative efforts to implement
those values.

14. Improve the accessibility of information about the United
Nations, its affiliated agencies, and their programs:

a) Make information user-friendly, more
accessible, and more timely.

b) Make better use of mass media to publicize,
popularize, and promote the principles,
goals, and programs of the U.N.

c) Prepare and distribute press releases on
current U.N. activities, publications, conferences, etc., tailored for high school, university, and local newspapers.

d) Work with NGOs to increase U.N. coverage
on local television and radio shows.

e)   Utilize communication technologies, such
as InterNet and TogetherNet, for public
access to U.N. policies and programs.

15.   Assist the general public and media to understand the
total U.N. system, e.g., that:

a)   the U.N. is more than the Security Council
and the General Assembly.

b)   peacekeeping is only one of the U.N.'s programs and responsibilities.

c)   the U.N.'s specialized agencies involve millions of people, including scientists and
NGOs, in successful regional programs that
focus on basic human needs.

16.   Disseminate, in popular form and language, the central analyses, conclusions, and recommendations of
basic U.N. documents and conferences to grassroots
groups and educational systems.

17.   Publish and distribute a list of electronic resources
that the U.N. offers.

18.   Collaborate with senior-citizen networks such as
Elderhostel to involve senior citizens and utilize their
experience and influence to inform the public.

19.   Use the U.N.'s fiftieth anniversary for an unprecedented review of where we stand in the world, where
we want to go, and how to get there.

20.   Establish a World Group of Eminent Persons to deal
with the way this planet should be governed (Stockholm Initiative).

21.   Establish a U.N. General Assembly Committee and
national committees in all member states to prepare
the celebration of the year 2000 and our entry into the
third millennium.

APPENDIX

The United Nations at Fifty: Recognizing the Achievements

The United Nations was established in the aftermath of a devastating war to help stabilize international relations and give peace a more secure foundation. Amid the threat of nuclear war and seemingly endless regional conflicts, peace-keeping has become an overriding concern of the United Nations. In the process, the activities of blue-helmeted peacekeepers have emerged as the most visible role associated with the world organization.

The United Nations, however, is much more than a peacekeeper and forum for conflict resolution. Often without attracting attention, the U.N. and its family of agencies are engaged in a vast array of work that touches every aspect of people's lives around the world: child survival and development, environmental protection, human rights, health and medical research, alleviation of poverty and economic development, agricultural development and fisheries, education, family planning, emergency and disaster relief, air and sea travel, peaceful uses of atomic energy, and labor and workers' rights. Here, in brief, as published by the Fiftieth Anniversary Secretariat of the United Nations, is a sampling of what the United Nations organizations have accomplished since 1945.

1. **Maintaining peace and security.** By deploying more than thirty-five peacekeeping forces and observer missions, the U.N. has been able to restore calm to allow the negotiating process to go forward while saving millions of people from becoming casualties of conflicts. There are presently sixteen active peacekeeping forces in operation.

2. **Making peace.** Since 1945, the U.N. has been credited with negotiating 172 peaceful settlements that have ended regional conflicts. Recent cases include an end to the Iran-Iraq war, the withdrawal of Soviet troops from Afghanistan, and an end to the civil war in El Salvador. The U.N. has used quiet diplomacy to avert over eighty imminent wars.

3. **Promoting democracy.** The U.N. has enabled people in over forty-five countries to participate in free and fair elections, including those held in Cambodia, El Salvador, Eritrea, Nicaragua, and South Africa. It has provided electoral advice, assistance, and monitoring of results.

4. **Promoting development.** The U.N. system has devoted more attention and resources to the promotion of the development of human skills and potentials than any other external assistance effort. The systems' annual disbursements, including loans and grants, amount to more than $10 billion. The U.N. Development Program (UNDP), in close cooperation with over 170 member states and other U.N. agencies, designs and implements projects for agriculture, industry, education, and the environment. It supports more than five thousand projects with a budget of $1.3 billion. It is the largest multilateral source of grant development assistance. The

World Bank, as the forefront in mobilizing support for developing countries worldwide, has alone loaned $333 billion for development projects since 1946.

5. Promoting human rights. Since adopting the Universal Declaration of Human Rights in 1948, the U.N. has helped enact more than eighty comprehensive agreements on political, civil, economic, social, and cultural rights. By investigating individual complaints of human rights abuses, the U.N. Human Rights Commission has focused world attention on cases of torture, disappearance, and arbitrary detention, and has generated international pressure to be brought on governments to improve their human rights records..

6. Protecting the environment. The U.N. has played a vital role in fashioning a global program designed to protect the environment. The "Earth Summit," the U.N. Conference on Environment and Development held in Rio de Janeiro in 1992, resulted in treaties on biodiversity and climate change, and adoption of "Agenda 21"—a program of action for sustainable development.

7. Preventing nuclear proliferation. The U.N., through the International Atomic Energy Agency, has helped minimize the threat of a nuclear war by inspecting nuclear reactors in ninety countries to ensure that nuclear materials are not diverted for military purposes.

8. Promoting self-determination and independence. The U.N. has played a pivotal role in bringing about independence in eighty countries that are now among its member states.

9. Strengthening international law. Over three hundred international treaties, on topics as varied as human rights conventions to agreements on the use of outer space, have been enacted through the efforts of the U.N.

10. Handing down judicial settlements of major international disputes. By giving judgments and advisory opinions, the International Court of Justice has helped settle international disputes involving territorial issues, non-interference in the internal affairs of states, diplomatic relations, hostage-taking, the right of asylum, rights of passage, and economic rights.

11. Ending apartheid in South Africa. By imposing measures ranging from an arms embargo to a convention against segregated sporting events, the U.N. played a major role in ending the apartheid system, which the General Assembly called "a crime against humanity." Elections in April 1994 allowed all South Africans to participate on an equal basis, and were followed by the establishment of a majority government.

12. Providing humanitarian aid to victims of conflict. More than 30 million refugees fleeing war, famine, or persecution have received aid from the U.N. High Commissioner for Refugees since 1951 in a continuing effort coordinated by the U.N. that often involves other agencies. There are more than 19 million refugees, primarily women and children, who are receiving food, shelter, medical aid, education, and repatriation assistance.

13. Aiding Palestinian refugees. Since 1950, the U.N. Relief and Works Agency (UNRWA) has sustained four generations of Palestinians with free schooling, essential health care, relief assistance, and key social services virtually without interruption. There are 2.9 million refugees in the Middle East served by UNRWA.

14. Alleviating chronic hunger and rural poverty in developing countries. The International Fund for Agricultural Development (IFAD) has developed a system of providing credit, often in very small amounts, for the poorest and most marginalized groups that has benefitted over 230 million people in nearly one hundred developing countries.

15. Focusing on African development. For the U.N., Africa continues to be the highest priority. In 1986, the U.N. convened a special session to generate international support for African economic recovery and development. The U.N. also has instituted a systemwide task force to ensure that commitments made by the international community are honored and challenges met. The Africa Project Development Facility has helped entrepreneurs in twenty-five countries find financing for new enterprises. The Facility has completed 130 projects which represent investments of $233 million and the creation of thirteen thousand new jobs. It is expected that these new enterprises will either earn or save some $131 million in foreign exchange annually.

16. Promoting women's rights. A long term objective of the U.N. has been to improve the lives of women and to empower women to have greater control over their lives. Several conferences during the U.N.-sponsored International Women's Decade set an agenda for the advancement of women and women's rights for the rest of the century. The U.N. Development Fund for Women (UNIFEM) and the International Research and Training Institute for the Advancement of Women (INSTRAW) have supported programs and projects to improve the quality of life for women in over one hundred countries. They include credit and training, access to new food-production technologies and marketing opportunities, and other means of promoting women's work.

17. Providing safe drinking water. U.N. agencies have worked to make safe drinking water available to 1.3 billion people in rural areas during the last decade.

18. Eradicating smallpox. A thirteen-year effort by the World Health Organization resulted in the complete eradication of small pox from the planet in 1980. The eradication has saved an estimated $1 billion a year in vaccination and monitoring, almost three times the cost of eliminating the scourge itself. WHO also helped wipe out polio from the Western hemisphere, with global eradication expected by the year 2000.

19. Pressing for universal immunization. Polio, tetanus, measles, whooping cough, diphtheria, and tuberculosis still kill more than eight million children each year. In 1974, only five percent of children in developing countries were immunized against these diseases. Today, as a result of the efforts of UNICEF and WHO, there is an eighty percent immunization rate, saving the lives of more than 3 million children each year.

20. Reducing child mortality rates. By providing water, sanitation, and other health and nutrition measures, the U.N. has been instrumental in decreasing child mortality rates in developing countries by half since 1960, increasing average life expectancy from thirty-seven to sixty-seven years.

21. Fighting parasitic diseases. Efforts by U.N. agencies in North Africa to eliminate the dreaded screw worm, a parasite that feeds on human and animal flesh, prevented the spread of the parasite, which is carried by flies, to Egypt, Tunisia, sub-Saharan Africa and Europe. A WHO program has saved 7 million children from river blindness and has rescued many others from guinea worm and other tropical diseases.

22. Promoting investment in developing countries. Through the efforts of the U.N. Industrial Development Organization (UNIDO), the U.N. has served as a "matchmaker" for North–South, and East–West investment, promoting entrepreneurship and self-reliance, industrial cooperation and technology transfer, and cost-effective, ecologically sensitive industry.

23. Orienting economic policy toward social need. Many U.N. agencies have emphasized taking account of human needs in determining economic adjustment and restructuring policies and programs, including measures to safeguard the poor.

24. Reducing the effects of natural disasters. The World Meteorological Organization (WMO) has spared millions of people from the calamitous effects of both natural and man-made disasters. Its early warning system, which utilizes thousands of surface monitors as well as satellites, has provided information for the dispersal of oil spills and has predicted long-term droughts. The system has allowed for the efficient distribution of food aid to drought regions, such as southern Africa in 1992.

25. Providing food to victims of emergencies. Over two million tons of food are distributed each year by the World Food Program (WFP). Nearly 30 million people facing acute food shortages in thirty-six countries benefited from this assistance in 1994.

26. Clearing land mines. The U.N. is leading an international effort to clear land mines from former battlefields in Afghanistan, Angola, Cambodia, El Salvador, Mozambique, Rwanda, and Somalia that still kill and maim thousands of innocent people every year.

27. Protecting the ozone layer. The U.N. Environment Program (UNEP) and the World Meteorological Organization (WMO) have been instrumental in highlighting the damage caused to the earth's ozone layer and in negotiating the Montreal Protocol to reduce emissions of chemical substances that cause the depletion of the ozone layer. The effort will spare millions of people from the increased risk of cancer due to additional exposure to ultraviolet radiation.

28. Curbing global warming. Through the Global Environment Facility (GEF), countries have contributed resources to curb the causes of global warming. Emissions from burning fossil fuels and changes in land use patterns have led to a buildup of gases in the atmosphere which experts believe can lead to a warming of the Earth's temperature.

29. Preventing overfishing. The Food and Agriculture Organization (FAC) monitors marine fishery production and issues alerts to prevent damage due to overfishing.

30. Limiting deforestation and promoting sustainable forestry development. FAO, UNDP, and the World Bank, through a Tropical Forests Action Program, have formulated and carried out forestry action plans in ninety countries.

31. Cleaning up pollution. UNEP led a major effort to clean up the Mediterranean Sea. It encouraged adversaries such as Syria and Israel, and Turkey and Greece to work together to clean up beaches. As a result, more than fifty percent of the previously polluted beaches are now usable.

32. Protecting consumers' health. To ensure the safety of food sold in the market place, U.N. agencies have established standards for over two hundred food commodities and safety limits for more than three thousand food contaminants.

33. Reducing fertility rates. The U.N. Population Fund (UNFPA), through its family planning programs, has enabled people to make informed choices, and consequently given families, and especially women, greater control over their lives. As a result, women in developing countries are having fewer children—from 6 births per woman in the 1960s to 3.5 today. In the 1960s, only 10 percent of the world's families were using effective methods of family planning. The number now stands at 55 percent.

34. Fighting drug abuse. The U.N. International Drug Control Program (UNDCP) has worked to reduce demand for illicit drugs, suppress drug trafficking, and helps farmers reduce their reliance on narcotic crops by shifting farm production toward other sources of income.

35. Improving global relations. The U.N. Conference on Trade and Development (UNCTAD) has worked to obtain special trade preferences for developing countries to export their products to developed countries. It has also negotiated international commodities agreements to ensure fair prices for developing countries. And through the General Agreement on Tariffs and Trade (GATT), which has now been supplanted by the World Trade Organization (WTO), the U.N. has supported trade liberalization aimed at increasing economic development opportunities in developing countries.

36. Promoting economic reform. Together with the World Bank and the International Monetary Fund, the U.N. has helped many countries improve their economic management, offered training for government finance officials, and provided financial assistance to countries experiencing temporary balance-of-payment difficulties.

37. Promoting worker rights. The International Labor Organization (ILO) has worked to guarantee freedom of association, the right to organize, collective bargaining, the rights of indigenous and tribal peoples. It has also promoted employment and equal remuneration, and has sought to eliminate discrimination and child labor. By setting safety standards, ILO has helped reduce work-related accidents.

38. Introducing improved agricultural techniques and reducing costs. With assistance from the Food and Agricultural Organization (FAO) that has resulted in improved crop yields, Asian rice farmers have saved $12 million on pesticides, and governments have saved over $150 million a year in pesticide subsidies.

39. Promoting stability and order in the world's oceans. Through three international conferences, the third lasting more than nine years, the U.N. has spearheaded an international effort to promote a comprehensive global agreement for the protection, preservation, and peaceful development of the oceans. The U.N. Convention on the Law of the Sea, which came into force in 1994, lays down rules for the determination of national maritime jurisdiction, navigation on the high seas, the rights and duties of coastal and other states, the obligation to protect and preserve the marine environment, cooperation in the conduct of scientific research, and the preservation of living resources.

40. Improving air and sea travel. U.N. agencies have been responsible for setting safety standards for sea and air travel. The efforts of the International Civil Aviation Organization (CIAO) have contributed to making air travel the safest mode of transportation. To wit: In 1947, when nine million traveled, 590 were killed in aircraft accidents; in 1993 the number of deaths was 936 out of the 1.2 billion airline passengers. In the last two decades, pollution from tankers has been reduced by as much as sixty percent due to the work of the International Maritime Organization (IMO).

41. Protecting intellectual property. The World Intellectual Property Organization (WIPO) provides protection for new inventions and maintains a register of nearly 3 million national trademarks. Through treaties, it also protects the works of artists, composers, and authors worldwide. WIPO's work makes it easier and less costly for individuals and enterprises to enforce their property rights. It also broadens the opportunity to distribute new ideas and products without relinquishing control over the property rights.

42. Promoting the free flow of information. To allow all people to obtain information that is free of censorship and culturally unbiased, UNESCO has provided aid to develop and strengthen communication systems, established news agencies, and supported an independent press.

43. Improving global communications. The Universal Postal Union (UPU) has maintained and regulated international mail delivery. The International Telecommunications Union (ITU) has coordinated use of the radio spectrum, promoted cooperation in assigning positions for stationary satellites, and established international standards for communication, thereby ensuring the unfettered flow of information around the globe.

44. Empowering the voiceless. U.N.-sponsored international years and conferences have caused governments to recognize the needs and contributions of groups usually excluded from decision-making, such as the aging, children, youth, homeless, and disabled people.

45. **Establishing "children as a zone of peace."** From El Salvador to Lebanon, from Sudan to former Yugoslavia, UNICEF pioneered the establishment of "Days of Tranquility" and the opening of "Corridors of Peace" to provide vaccines and other assistance desperately needed by children caught in armed conflict.

46. **Generating worldwide commitment in support of the needs of children.** Through UNICEF's efforts, the Convention on the Rights of the Child entered into force in 1990 and became law in 166 countries by the end of September 1994. Following the 1990 World Summit for Children convened by UNICEF, more than 150 governments committed themselves to attain twenty specific goals to radically improve children's lives by the year 2000.

47. **Improving education in developing countries.** As a direct result of the efforts of U.N. agencies, over 60 percent of adults in developing countries can now read and write, and 80 percent of children in these countries attend school.

48. **Improving literacy for women.** Programs aimed at promoting education and advancement for women helped raise the female literacy rate in developing countries from 36 percent in 1970 to 56 percent in 1990.

49. **Safeguarding and preserving historic cultural and architectural sites.** Ancient monuments in eighty-one countries including Greece, Egypt, Italy, Indonesia and Cambodia have been protected through the efforts of UNESCO, and international conventions have been adopted to preserve cultural property.

50. **Facilitating academic and cultural exchanges.** The U.N., through UNESCO and the U.N. University (UNU), have encouraged scholarly and scientific cooperation, the networking of institutions, and the promotion of cultural expressions, including those of minorities and indigenous people.

ROBERT MULLER

$\mathcal{R}$obert Muller served the United Nations for thirty-eight years until his retirement as a high-ranking officer in 1986. An internationally known speaker and author, he is Chancellor-Emeritus of the University for Peace, established by the U.N. in Costa Rica.

During the last sixteen years of his career, Robert Muller worked directly with three secretaries-general, U Thant, Kurt Waldheim and Javier Perez de Cuellar, as director of the secretary-general's office, as secretary of the Economic and Social Council and as deputy under-secretary-general for coordination and interagency affairs in the secretary-general's office. In this capacity he helped coordinate the work of the thirty-two U.N. specialized agencies and world programs. He was also in charge of launching several world conferences and international years. Appointed assistant secretary-general by Perez de Cuellar, his last assignment at the U.N. was to organize the fortieth anniversary of the U.N. in 1985.

His books have been published in several languages. These include *New Genesis: Shaping a Global Spirituality; What War Taught Me About Peace; Peace Plan 2010; Au bonheur, l'amour, la paix*; and the novels *First Lady of the World* and *Sima mon amour*, a multicultural novel unfolding in the U.N., in France and India, which received the 1983 Erckmann-Chatrian literary prize.

He is considered the father of global education, and his World Core Curriculum is used in an increasing number of schools around the world and serves as the educational structure of several Robert Muller Schools.

Muller received the 1989 UNESCO Peace Education Prize, the 1993 International Albert Schweitzer Prize for Humanities, and the 1994 Eleanor Roosevelt Man of Vision Award.

DOUGLAS ROCHE

*A*uthor, parliamentarian and diplomat, Douglas Roche was Canada's Ambassador for Disarmament, 1984–1989. He was elected chairman of the United Nations Disarmament Committee in 1988.

Roche was elected to the Canadian Parliament four times, serving from 1972 to 1984, and specializing in the subjects of development and disarmament. He lectures widely on these themes.

He is the author of twelve books, including *Justice Not Charity: A New Global Ethic for Canada* and *United Nations: Divided World*. His most recent book is *A Bargain for Humanity: Global Security By 2000* (University of Alberta Press, 1993).

Roche has served as president of the United Nations Association in Canada, and was named chairman of the Canadian Committee for the Fiftieth Anniversary of the United Nations. He was the founding president of Parliamentarians for Global Action, and founding editor of the *Western Catholic Reporter*.

An Honorary Doctor of Divinity was awarded him by St. Stephen's College, Edmonton. He has also received Honorary Doctor of Laws degrees from Simon Fraser University and the University of Alberta. In 1992, he was given the Thakore Foundation Award "in recognition of his prolonged and distinguished work towards disarmament, global peace and peace education."

In 1989, Roche was appointed visiting professor at the University of Alberta, where he teaches "War and Peace in the 1990s." He serves as Special Advisor on disarmament and security matters on the Holy See's delegation to the U.N. General Assembly. He was elected international chairman of Global Education Associates, New York and received an Honorary Doctor of Humane Letters from St. Peter's College, Jersey City, N.J., for his work at the United Nations. In 1992, he was named an Officer of the Order of Canada.